THE AUTHENTIC GILBERT & SULLIVAN SONGBOOK

92 Unabridged Selections from All 14 Operas
Reproduced from Early Vocal Scores

Collected by
MALCOLM BINNEY and PETER LAVENDER

Selected and with Plot Summaries by
JAMES SPERO

Dover Publications, Inc., New York

PUBLISHER'S NOTE

The songs in the collection have been reproduced from early vocal scores authorized by Sir Arthur Sullivan himself. Savoyards may notice that there are a few instances where lyrics differ slightly from the texts as they are performed today.

ILLUSTRATIONS

Frontispiece: Gilbert (right) and Sullivan (left) as caricatured by E. J. Wheeler in *Punch*, March 28, 1885, two weeks after the opening of *The Mikado* at the Savoy.

Page iv: Illustration by Gilbert for *Songs of a Savoyard* (see "The Law is the true embodiment," p. 153).

Page xi: Illustration by Gilbert for the Bab Ballad "The Bumboat Woman's Story," one of his earlier works upon which he drew for material for *H.M.S. Pinafore*.

Published in Canada by General Publishing Company,
Ltd., 30 Lesmill Road, Don Mills, Toronto, Ontario.

The Authentic Gilbert & Sullivan Songbook is a new work,
first published by Dover Publications, Inc., in 1977.

International Standard Book Number: 0-486-23482-7
Library of Congress Catalog Card Number: 76-55957

Manufactured in the United States of America
Dover Publications, Inc.
180 Varick Street
New York, N. Y. 10014

CONTENTS

(The place and date of the premiere of each operetta are listed after its title.)

PLOT SUMMARIES

(For full title and information on premieres, see Contents, p. iii)

Thespis

Thespis, the first operetta on which Gilbert and Sullivan collaborated, can never be revived for, with the exception of two numbers, the score is lost. The plot involves an ancient Athenian theatrical troupe picnicking on Mount Olympus. There they meet the gods, who have grown old and feeble. The gods go to spend a year on earth, leaving the Thespians to rule in their stead. The results are disastrous and the gods resume their proper places. "Little maid of Arcadee" survives because it was published as sheet music. The song is delivered by Sparkeion, one of Thespis' troupe, as an attempt to cheer up a friend suffering from troubles of the heart. (The other surviving number is the chorus "Climbing over rocky mountain" which, with a slight change of lyrics, was used again in *The Pirates of Penzance*.)

Trial by Jury

The action of this, the only Gilbert and Sullivan one-acter (commissioned to fill out an evening featuring Offenbach's *La Périchole*), is set in a court of justice. Edwin, who has left Angelina waiting at the altar, is being tried for breach of promise of marriage. Before the trial begins, he explains the reasons for his change of heart ("When first my old, old love I knew"). The Judge enters, takes everyone into his confidence, and tells the tale of his legal career ("When I, good friends, was call'd to the bar"). The trial commences. Angelina enters, still wearing her bridal gown and attended by bridesmaids. The Counsel for the Plaintiff pleads her case most effectively ("With a sense of deep emotion"), and opinion is roused against Edwin, who offers a compromise—he will marry Angelina that day, and his new flame the next ("O gentlemen, listen I pray"). All are agreeable until the Counsel for the Plaintiff points out that that would be bigamy. The situation has reached an impasse. The Judge hits on a plan that saves the day—he will marry Angelina himself. The trial is over.

The Sorcerer

The first act is set in the garden of Sir Marmaduke Pointdextre's mansion in the village of Ploverleigh. The villagers are assembled to celebrate the betrothal of Alexis, Sir Marmaduke's son, to Aline, daughter of Lady Sangazure. The vicar, Dr. Daly, pines for the days of his youth, when feminine breasts beat for him alone ("Time was, when Love and I"). The parties arrive for the ceremony. Sir Marmaduke and Lady Sangazure, who had been madly in love fifty years previously, exchange old-fashioned, courtly compliments ("Welcome joy! adieu to sadness!"). Their children, by contrast, throw themselves at each other with passionate abandon. The marriage contract, delivered by the decrepit Notary, is signed, witnessed and sealed. But Alexis is not perfectly happy. Everyone, he feels, should experience the glory of true and lasting love. To insure that the entire village may know it, he has sent for the distinguished merchant-sorcerer, John Wellington Wells, who has in stock (among other things) an extremely effective love potion. The business-like sorcerer enters and introduces himself ("My name is John Wellington Wells"). At Alexis' request, he slips the love philter into the teapot and it is served to the unsuspecting villagers, who drink and fall insensible. In the second act the villagers awaken to find that it is night. True to the potion's peculiar power, each falls in love with the first person he sees—with catastrophic results. Mrs. Partlet, an elderly pew-opener, pairs off with Sir Marmaduke. Mrs. Partlet's young daughter, Constance, cannot understand why she has suddenly conceived a passion for the Notary ("Dear friends, take pity on my lot"). Wells himself is horrified to find that Lady Sangazure is now infatuated with him. At the urging of Alexis, Aline takes the potion so that they may be certain of each other's eternal love. By accident, however, the first person Aline sees is Dr. Daly. Things have gotten completely out of hand. Only the sacrifice of Mr. Wells will break the potion's hold over the village. As the villagers turn their attention to the belated betrothal banquet, the obliging John Wellington Wells sinks into the ground amid fire and smoke.

H.M.S. Pinafore

The setting is the quarterdeck of the H.M.S. *Pinafore*, off Portsmouth. As the curtain rises, sailors are seen going about their business ("We sail the ocean blue"). Little Buttercup enters to sell some of the wares she peddles from ship to ship ("I'm called little Buttercup"). One of the sailors, Ralph Rackstraw, moons over his hopeless love for Josephine, daughter of his commander, Captain Corcoran ("A maiden fair to see"). How can he, a mere able-bodied seaman, dream of crossing class lines to marry her? Captain Corcoran enters and bids the assembled crew good morning ("I am the captain of the *Pinafore*"). All make ready for the arrival of Sir Joseph Porter, First Lord of the Admiralty, who is coming to claim Josephine's hand. Josephine confesses to her father that, although she loves a seaman on board his own ship, she will show her breeding and marry Sir

Joseph. The First Lord arrives, attended by his sisters, female cousins and aunts ("I am the monarch of the sea"). He tells of his rise to his exalted position ("When I was a lad"). The crowd moves off. Josephine reenters. Sir Joseph's attentions only nauseate her. Seeing her alone, Ralph decides to declare his love. Although thrilled, Josephine pretends to be horrified and spurns him. Only when Ralph threatens suicide does she reveal her true feelings. Aided by Sir Joseph's relatives and members of the crew, the happy pair plan to elope. That evening Sir Joseph tells the Captain that he is not satisfied with Josephine —she does not seem responsive to him. The Captain reasons that she is probably cowed by his station. Unwittingly strengthening Josephine's resolve, the two men explain to her that love is a leveler of all ranks ("Never mind the why and wherefore"). The elopement, however, is disrupted by Captain Corcoran, who has been forewarned by Dick Deadeye, a disgruntled member of the crew. The Boatswain tries to defend Ralph ("He is an Englishman!") but the Captain works himself into a towering rage and hurls an oath at the poor seaman just as Sir Joseph enters. The First Lord, a gentleman to his fingertips, is appalled at such bad language, and sends the Captain out. But when he learns of Ralph's relationship with Josephine, he orders the seaman placed in irons. Little Buttercup saves the day by telling of how, when young, she nursed two infants and switched them by mistake. The two babes were—of course—the Captain and Ralph. Since Sir Joseph cannot marry the daughter of a common sailor (love does not level ranks as much as that), he decides to wed Hebe, one of his cousins. Ralph and Josephine are now free to marry and the Captain finds consolation in Little Buttercup. With the prospect of a triple wedding, the curtain falls.

The Pirates of Penzance

The first act takes place along a rocky beach on the coast of Cornwall. A pirate band are celebrating the 21st birthday of Frederick, who is just ending his term of indenture to them. When a babe, he had been apprenticed to them by his nurse Ruth, who, being a bit deaf, had misunderstood his father's request that he be apprenticed to a *pilot*. Realizing her mistake, she has remained with the pirates. Frederick admits that, while he loves the pirates individually, he loathes them collectively and that once free he will devote his energies to their eradication. The Pirate King defends his calling ("Oh, better far to live and die"). The pirates move off. Frederick hides when he sees a picnic party of beautiful girls—the daughters of Major-General Stanley—approach. Frederick reveals himself to them and begs for one—any one—to marry him. None responds save Mabel ("Poor wand'ring one!"). The pirates return and seize the girls. The Major-General enters ("I am the very model of a

modern Major-General"). Taking advantage of the one known soft spot of these dreaded pirates, he pleads falsely that he is an orphan. The men, all orphans themselves, would not dream of depriving him of his daughters, who are returned to him. That night, in a ruined chapel on his estate, the Major-General broods over the lie he told. Frederick attempts to calm him. The local constabulary has been sent for; they will march against the pirates. Led by the Sergeant, the timid policemen enter ("When the foeman bares his steel"). The police and the somewhat bloodthirsty girls leave Frederick alone. The Pirate King and Ruth slip in. They have discovered an anomaly ("When you had left our pirate fold"). Frederick had been apprenticed until he reached his 21st *birthday*—but he was born on a February 29th! This means that he will not be out of his indenture until 1940. Since he is thus still a member of the band, his sense of duty forces him to reveal the Major-General's lie. The Pirate King is enraged. The Pirates will attack immediately and exact terrible vengeance. Mabel, told of what has happened, calls upon the police. The Sergeant laments his lot ("When a felon's not engaged in his employment"). The police hide when the pirates enter ("With cat-like tread"). The pirates pounce on the unsuspecting Major-General. The police leap upon the pirates, but are quickly bested. Only quick thinking by the Sergeant saves the lives of his men and the Major-General: he commands the pirates to surrender in the name of Queen Victoria, and they obey instantaneously. Ruth rushes in to reveal that all the pirates are really noblemen who have gone wrong. That being the case, the Major-General bids them wed his daughters.

Patience

Patience is a satire on Oscar Wilde, James Whistler, Algernon Swinburne and the whole aesthetic movement. The curtain rises on the exterior of Castle Bunthorne. A chorus of lovesick maidens are mooning about, lamenting the lack of interest shown in them by the aesthetic poet Reginald Bunthorne. He is interested only in Patience, a milkmaid who cares nothing for him. Patience enters and tells them that she has never felt love ("I cannot tell what this love may be"). The women drift into the castle to serenade their idol. Officers of the dragoon guards enter, led by Colonel Calverley ("If you want a receipt"). They have come to call upon the ladies, whom they have not seen in months. How shocked they are to see them in their bizarre garb escorting the willowy Bunthorne in! Worse still, the maidens give their former beaux the cold shoulder. Bunthorne reads a poem. The women drift off in ecstasies; the dragoons storm off in disgust. Alone, Bunthorne confesses that his pose is a sham ("Am I alone, And unobserved?"). In converse with one of the aesthetic maidens, Patience puzzles over love. She is told that *true* love is completely unselfish. Patience does remember having felt that emotion for a little playmate when she was four. A stranger in aesthetic garb—Archibald Grosvenor—enters and proposes to Patience ("Prithee, pretty maiden"). He is the babe for whom she had felt love and he has grown into a handsome and infallible poet—he can do no wrong. They decide to marry but to her horror Patience realizes that to monopolize so beautiful a creature as Grosvenor would be selfish, so her love cannot be true. They cannot wed. Bunthorne is led on by the maidens like a sheep to slaughter. Despairing of Patience's love, he is putting himself up to be raffled for. The proceedings are interrupted by Patience. Since there could be nothing selfish about loving someone as unpleasant as Bunthorne, she will marry him after all. The ladies are furious until Archibald strolls on. They immediately attach themselves to him. The dragoons, once again, are left out in the cold. The second act, set in a glade, is opened by the elderly Lady Jane, who, alone of the maidens, has remained loyal to Bunthorne. Accompanying herself on the cello, she sings of her fast-fading charms ("Sad is that woman's lot"). A weary Grosvenor tries to satisfy the women, who trail him constantly, with a song ("A magnet hung in a hardware shop"). Bunthorne is wretched; it is obvious that Patience does not love him and he has also lost his female entourage. Lady Jane advises him to confront Grosvenor—the county is big enough for only one poet ("So go to him"). Threatened by Bunthorne's terrible curse, Grosvenor promises to give up aestheticism entirely ("When I go out of door"). But Bunthorne's triumph is short-lived—the ladies troop back on, divested of aesthetic garb, wearing regular daytime clothing. Archibald the All-Right has discarded aestheticism, which means that aestheticism *ought* to be discarded. Patience is free to marry Grosvenor, the dragoons are reunited with their ladies, and Bunthorne—deserted even by Lady Jane—is left brideless.

Iolanthe

The first act is set in an Arcadian landscape. A chorus of fairies dances in ("Tripping hither, tripping thither"). They are sad, for they miss Iolanthe, who was banished to the bottom of a nearby pond for having married a mortal (usually a capital offense). The fairies plead with their Queen to pardon her, and she relents. Iolanthe is reinstated to their number. Iolanthe's son, Strephon the shepherd, greets his mother and the fairies. He tells them that he loves the shepherdess Phyllis, who is a ward in Chancery. Although he has been unable to secure the Lord Chancellor's permission, he plans to marry Phyllis that very day. He has, however, told her nothing of his fairyhood; she might misconstrue it. The peers of the realm enter in full regalia, led by the Earls Tolloller and Mountararat ("Loudly let the trumpet bray"). The Lord Chancellor enters ("The Law is the true embodiment"). The peers have come as suitors, but Phyllis disappoints them—she will not marry a peer, for the peerage is bereft of virtue. Lord Tolloller vainly tries to rectify her views ("Spurn not the nobly born"). The peers are shocked when Strephon claims Phyllis. The Lord Chancellor denies permission again and gives Strephon some advice ("When I went to the Bar"). Iolanthe, finding her son alone and heartbroken, tries to console him. The two are spied by Phyllis. Not realizing that the attractive lady is really her beau's mother (for fairies are eternally youthful), she jilts Strephon and announces that she will marry one of the peers—she doesn't care which. In despair Strephon calls on his fairy aunts, who flutter in. Angered by the peers, the Fairy Queen casts a spell that will put Strephon in Parliament. The second act takes place in Palace Yard, Westminster, at night. Private Willis, a guard, whiles away the time ("When all night long a chap remains"). The angered peers march in from a night session of the House of Lords. Strephon is succeeding in his reforms of the House, and they resent it. Lord Mountararat sings of better times ("When Britain really rul'd the waves"). The fairies enter. They have become quite fond of the peers. *Too* fond, says the Fairy Queen, herself smitten by Willis ("Oh, foolish fay"). The Lord Chancellor staggers in, haggard from loss of sleep caused by love of Phyllis ("Love, unrequited"). Lords Tolloller and Mountararat urge him to press his suit ("If you go in"). Strephon reveals his fairyhood to Phyllis and the pair is reunited. The Lord Chancellor, however, announces his intention of marrying his ward. But the Lord Chancellor's wife, long thought dead, still lives. She is Iolanthe! To prevent bigamy Iolanthe reveals herself to her husband, even though this means certain death. The Fairy Queen is about to plunge her spear into Iolanthe's breast when the Lord Chancellor stops her. Why not change fairy law so that every fairy must die who does *not* marry a mortal? A capital idea! To save their lives, the fairies marry the peers, and the Fairy Queen marries Willis. The peers and the fairy guardsman sprout little wings and the entire crew flies off to Fairyland, where the peers really belong.

Princess Ida

The first act takes place on the grounds of King Hildebrand's palace. The court, along with Hildebrand's son Hilarion and his two companions Cyril and Florian, await the arrival of King Gama. The king is to bring his daughter Ida, who was betrothed to Hilarion when a babe of one. Gama's three warrior sons, Arac, Guron and Scynthius, come on, followed by the acerb, querulous king ("If you give me your attention"). He bears bad news. Ida has holed herself up in Castle Adamant, where she runs a women's college. No male—of any species—is allowed there. Hilarion and his companions decide they will mount their own assault against the castle ("Expressive glances"). Gama and his sons are tossed into Hildebrand's dungeons as hostages. The second act is set in the gardens of Castle Adamant. The chorus of girl graduates has assembled to listen to Princess Ida lecture. Lady Blanche, Professor of Abstract Science, broods. She feels *she* should run the school. Hilarion, Cyril and Florian slip over the wall, find some academic gowns and disguise themselves as women ("I am a maiden"). Completely taken in, Ida admits them into her school. Lady Psyche, Professor of Humanities, recognizes her brother, Florian. She tells why Man is an ape at heart ("A Lady fair"). The four are discovered by Melissa, daughter of Lady Blanche, who immediately feels tremendous attraction towards these, the only members of the opposite sex she has ever seen. Lady Blanche spots the imposture, but Melissa persuades her to keep quiet, holding out the hope that the school will go to Blanche if Ida marries Hilarion. All the girls troop on for a picnic luncheon. Cyril, however, gets drunk and sings a spicy song ("Would you know the kind of maid"). The men's disguise is penetrated and in the ensuing confusion, Ida falls into a stream. She is saved from drowning by Hilarion, but shows no mercy. She orders the three bound—their lives are forfeit. Just then the castle gate is battered down by Hildebrand, who storms in. If Ida does not marry Hilarion, he will slaughter her brothers and sack the castle. Ida refuses to yield and makes ready for battle. The third act takes place along the outer walls and courtyard of the castle. The girls are running into trouble with their military preparations. What was simple in theory proves difficult for feminine hands in practice. Gama comes in, completely miserable. He has suffered an excruciating torture at the hands of Hildebrand—he has been treated so politely that he has nothing to complain about ("Whene'er I spoke"). He bears a proposal from Hildebrand. Rather than join in full battle, let a combat between Gama's sons and Hilarion, Cyril and Florian decide the issue. It is agreed. Arac, Guron and Scynthius make ready ("This helmet, I suppose"). They are beaten, and Ida surrenders, lamenting that posterity will now see her in an unfavorable light. Hildebrand is quick to point out that if she had had her way, there would have been no posterity at all. Irrefutable logic sends her into Hilarion's arms.

The Mikado

The first act is set in the courtyard of Ko-Ko's palace in Titipu, Japan. Nanki-Poo enters and introduces himself to the chorus of nobles ("A wand'ring minstrel, I"). He inquires after Yum-Yum, a young girl he had met there the year before. His passion for her was in vain, for she was engaged to Ko-Ko, the cheap tailor. Nanki-Poo has heard that Ko-Ko has been condemned to death under the Mikado's law against flirting, and so has hurried back to try to claim Yum-Yum. But the situation has changed. To circumvent the distasteful law, the town made Ko-Ko Lord High Executioner, reasoning that he would first have to cut off his own head before he could cut off anyone else's. The idea of serving under Ko-Ko was so repulsive to the nobles that they all resigned except fat, venal and pompous Pooh-Bah, who is performing all their official functions. Ko-Ko enters ("Behold the Lord High Executioner!") and tells of a list of potential victims which he keeps on hand ("As some day it may happen"). Attended by her friends Pitti-Sing and Peep-Bo, Yum-Yum enters ("Three little maids"). The girls slight Pooh-Bah's bloated sense of dignity ("So please you, Sir"). Left alone with Yum-Yum, Nanki-Poo confesses that he is really the son of the Mikado. He has fled his father's court to avoid marrying the elderly, ugly and bloodthirsty Katisha. But Yum-Yum, still engaged to Ko-Ko, must turn him down. Ko-Ko receives a letter from the Mikado, who has been alarmed by the town's lack of executions. An execution must take place soon, or Titipu will feel his wrath. Just then Nanki-Poo appears, a noose around his neck. Miserable at the thought of life without Yum-Yum, he is about to commit suicide. Ko-Ko works out an arrangement with him: if he is bent on self-destruction, then let him die at the hands of the Lord High Executioner. Nanki-Poo agrees only when Ko-Ko promises to allow him to marry Yum-Yum and enjoy a month of wedded bliss with her. After the execution, the widowed Yum-Yum will be free to marry Ko-Ko and everyone will be happy. All rejoice. But Katisha barges in. She is about to reveal Nanki-Poo's true identity, when the crowd, led by Pitti-Sing, silences her ("For he's going to marry Yum-Yum"). Frustrated and threatening vengeance, Katisha departs. The second act is set in Ko-Ko's garden. Yum-Yum admires herself as she prepares her bridal toilet ("The sun whose rays"). The wedding party assembles ("Brightly dawns our wedding day"). Ko-Ko enters with disturbing news. He has found that, by law, when a man is executed, his wife is buried alive ("Here's a how-de-do!"). Yum-Yum bows out of the marriage, and Nanki-Poo asks Ko-Ko to execute him on the spot. Ko-Ko's nerve fails him. Pooh-Bah announces that the Mikado is approaching Titipu. In terror, Ko-Ko fills out a false certificate of execution and tells Nanki-Poo to leave the country with Yum-Yum. The citizens of Titipu greet the Mikado ("Miya sama"), who explains his policies ("A more humane Mikado"). When Ko-Ko presents the certificate of execution, the Mikado is surprised to find that the victim was none other than his son. Murder of the heir apparent is a crime punishable by death. The Mikado goes off to have lunch, leaving Ko-Ko, Pitti-Sing and Pooh-Bah to await death by boiling oil or melted lead. The three catch Nanki-Poo as he and Yum-Yum are about to leave and beg him to present himself to his father. He refuses to do so unless Ko-Ko marries Katisha ("The flowers that bloom in the spring"). Katisha laments the supposed death of Nanki-Poo ("Alone, and yet alive!"). Ko-Ko woos her ("On a tree by a river") and wins her ("There is beauty in the bellow of the blast"). She is furious when she learns of his deception, but relents and begs the Mikado to pardon the whole crew. Completely confused by her actions and Ko-Ko's logic, he agrees.

Ruddigore
This is a parody of the blood-and-thunder melodramas that held the boards in the earlier part of the nineteenth century. The first act is set in the fishing village of Rederring in Cornwall during the Napoleonic wars. A chorus of professional bridesmaids stand in front of the cottage of Rose Maybud, the last eligible maiden in the village. They beg her to marry someone. Dame Hannah enters and tells them that they wait in vain. When the bridesmaids ask Hannah why she has never wed, she tells that she once loved one of the bad baronets of Ruddigore, Sir Roderick Murgatroyd, but could not face marrying one of his kind. The baronets had been cursed by a witch centuries before. Each must commit one crime a day or die in agony—eventually conscience manifests itself and they die. She jilted Roderick; he later died. Rose enters, and explains why she cannot find a beau ("If somebody there chanced to be"). She is, however, much infatuated with Robin Oakapple, a young farmer. Richard Dauntless, a mariner, enters and tells the bridesmaids of his exploits ("I shipped, d'ye see"). Robin, his half-brother, confesses to him that he loves Rose, but is much too shy to court her ("My boy, you may take it from me"). Richard volunteers to woo Rose for Robin, but when he starts he falls in love with her and takes her for himself. After deliberation among the three, Rose decides on Robin. Mad Margaret enters ("Cheerily carols the lark over the cot"). She lost her mind when Sir Despard, the present baronet, trifled with her affections. Attended by bucks and blades, Sir Despard enters. For his daily crime he is going to abduct Rose. Richard interrupts him to reveal that Robin is actually Sir Ruthven Murgatroyd, Sir Despard's elder brother, who is not dead, as had been thought. He had fled years ago to escape the family curse. Sir Despard disrupts the bridal party and charges Robin with his deception. Relieved of the title and curse, Despard is free to marry Margaret. Rose cannot possibly wed a wicked baronet and gives herself to Richard. The second act is set in the picture gallery of Ruddigore Castle. Robin has assumed the name of Sir Ruthven and the dreaded title. But his crimes have been petty ones, and as he stands alone in the gallery the portraits of his ancestors come to life and step down from their frames. The last to descend is Sir Roderick, who describes a ghost's life ("When the night wind howls"). Ruthven is then tormented until he promises to commit a first-rate crime, whereupon the ghosts return to their places. Robin orders Old Adam, his valet, to carry off any one of the village maidens so she can be held hostage at the castle. Despard and Margaret enter, scarcely recognizable. Both have become thoroughly respectable ("I once was a very abandoned person"). They persuade Ruthven to defy the ghosts ("My eyes are fully open"). Old Adam enters; he has carried off Dame Hannah. The crusty old woman is about to run Ruthven through with a dagger when Sir Roderick appears and is unexpectedly reunited with his old love. Ruthven has an inspiration. Refusal to commit a crime is tantamount to suicide, but suicide is itself a crime! Sir Roderick comes back to life and marries Hannah. Ruthven, no longer a bad bart., takes Rose. Richard finds a port in the storm by marrying Zorah, one of the bridesmaids.

The Yeomen of the Guard
The action takes place on the Tower Green of the Tower of London during the reign of Henry VIII. Phoebe, daughter of Sergeant Meryll of the Yeomen, laments the impending execution of Colonel Fairfax. The charges against him were trumped up by a relative seeking his estate. Phoebe has lost her heart to the doomed man ("When maiden loves"). She rejects the advances of the odious Wilfred Shadbolt, Head Jailor and Assistant Tormentor. Phoebe's brother Leonard is to join the Yeomen that day for having rendered distinguished service in battle. Leonard slips in and, with Sergeant Meryll and Phoebe, forms a plan to save Fairfax. They will engineer his escape and, his beard shaven, they will introduce him as "Leonard" while the real Leonard stays hidden. With luck that should keep Fairfax alive until a pardon comes through. As they exit, Fairfax enters, accepting his fate philosophically ("Is life a boon?"). He asks one favor of his old friend, the Lieutenant of the Tower. He wants to marry any willing maiden who can be found, so that his estate will pass to her, thus spiting his scheming relative. A crowd enters jostling two strolling players, the jester Jack Point and his fiancée Elsie Maynard. They sing to appease the mob ("I have a song to sing, O!"). The Lieutenant approaches Elsie and urges her to marry Fairfax, who has been returned to his cell. At first both she and Point are loathe to comply, but the Lieutenant holds out the promise of 100 crowns and immediate widowhood. Since Elsie's mother is in need of expensive medicine, they agree. Elsie is blindfolded and led out to be married, while Point tries to secure a position as jester with the Lieutenant ("I've jibe and joke"). Now Phoebe plays up to Wilfred just long enough to slip the key to Fairfax's cell out of his keyring, give it to

her father and replace it after Fairfax has been smuggled out ("Were I thy bride"). Citizens and Yeomen gather to greet the bogus Leonard, who is accepted without suspicion. A tolling bell announces the time for Fairfax's execution. Guards rush on, having discovered the escape. Shadbolt is disgraced and Elsie, now married to Fairfax and thus no longer free to marry Point, collapses. The second act takes place in the evening, two days later. A thorough combing of the Tower has failed to turn up a trace of Fairfax. Point laments his state ("Oh! a private buffoon"). Shadbolt commiserates with him. Then Point has an idea which may free Elsie for him. Let Shadbolt claim—falsely—that he has shot Fairfax dead as he tried to escape by swimming the Thames. In return Point will fulfill Shadbolt's greatest ambition by teaching him how to be a jester. The pact is made. Dame Carruthers, housekeeper to the Tower, tells her niece Kate, Sergeant Meryll and "Leonard" that Elsie has been talking in her sleep and has revealed her marriage ("Strange adventure!"). "Leonard," who had also been blindfolded at the marriage ceremony, is delighted to learn that Elsie is his bride; he has fallen in love with her. Elsie feels a similar attraction but cannot acknowledge it, for she is married to a stranger—a man she imagines to be a monster. Wilfred announces his pretended slaying of Fairfax: now Elsie is free, but must choose between Point and "Leonard." Point is instructed in the art of wooing ("A man who would woo a fair maid"). "Leonard" wins Elsie, to the consternation of Phoebe and Point ("When a wooer Goes a-wooing"). To silence Wilfred, who has discovered "Leonard's" true identity and threatens to jeopardize his happiness, Phoebe self-sacrificingly promises to marry the jailor. In a similar situation, Meryll agrees to marry Dame Carruthers. A wedding procession forms, Carruthers with Meryll, and Elsie awaiting "Leonard." The Lieutenant interrupts to announce that Fairfax has been pardoned. At first Elsie despairs, but she exults when she discovers that "Leonard" and Fairfax are the same. All rejoice save Point who, heartbroken, falls insensible.

The Gondoliers

The first act is set in the Piazzetta, Venice, 1750. A chorus of *contadine* (peasant girls) prepare to greet the two most popular and desirable gondoliers in Venice, Marco and Giuseppe Palmieri. The brothers are on their way to choose two of the girls as their brides. They enter ("We're called *gondolieri*"). Having selected Tessa and Gianetta, they go off to be married. A gondola pulls up and out step the Duke of Plaza Toro (a Grandee of Spain), his Duchess, his daughter Casilda and attendant Luiz. Their old, faded clothes indicate their poverty. The Duke tells of his military career ("In enterprise of martial kind").

When a babe, Casilda had been married by proxy to the infant son of the King of Barataria. The child was spirited away by the Inquisition for safekeeping. The old King has just been assassinated and Casilda has been brought to Venice where Don Alhambra del Bolero, the Grand Inquisitor, dwells. He will deliver her to the new King, and the pair will go off to rule Barataria. Casilda is less than thrilled by the prospect, for she secretly loves lowly Luiz. Don Alhambra comes on and confesses that a snag has arisen. When he brought the infant to Venice, he had entrusted him to a gondolier who had a child of his own ("I stole the Prince"). The gondolier, a heavy drinker, soon mixed the two babes up, so the precise identity of the new King is not quite clear. But things will soon be set straight, for the infant's old nurse is still alive in Spain. She will be sent for, and will identify the rightful ruler. As fate would have it, the King is one of the Palmieri brothers, who just then reenter, having wed their brides ("When a merry maiden marries"). Don Alhambra informs them that one of them is now a King and that, since Barataria has immediate need of a monarch, they must go there at once and rule jointly. The brothers manage to reconcile the new post with their strong republican principles, while their wives are delighted ("Then one of us will be a Queen"). Don Alhambra dampens the ladies' spirits by telling them that they must remain behind. The two brothers depart with their fellow gondoliers for the island kingdom. The second act is set in a pavilion in the court of Barataria. The two brothers have put their republican theories into practice. Drummer boys and footmen hobnob with courtiers and officers of rank. But the men miss the company of the women they have left behind ("Take a pair of sparkling eyes"). The ladies burst onto the scene—they have come because they could bear the separation no longer. All break into a mad dance ("Dance a cachucha"). Don Alhambra's entrance puts a sudden end to their cavorting. He tries to explain why their republican reforms are doomed to failure ("There lived a King"). He further distresses them by revealing that either Marco or Giuseppe is married to Casilda. The Duke and Duchess enter, gorgeously dressed. The Duke has incorporated himself, and turns in a handsome profit. He instructs Marco and Giuseppe in aristocratic bearing ("I am a courtier grave and serious"). The situation seems hopelessly entangled. Who is the King? And who is married to him? And what will happen to the superfluous wife? The King's aged nurse is brought on, a session in the torture chamber having jogged her memory, and she identifies the King. It was her own son who was given to the gondolier; and it was the King she passed off for all these years as her son. He is Luiz! Luiz and Casilda are royally united; the two gondoliers, still wed to the women they love, are free to return to Venice. On a reprise of the cachucha, the curtain falls.

Utopia, Limited

Overly contrived and showing signs of flagging inspiration by both composer and librettist, this operetta has had few professional revivals since its initial run. Briefly, the plot concerns a balmy island, Utopia, in the South Seas. The king's daughter returns after five years in England. With the aid of six Englishmen (the Imported Flowers of Progress), the happy island is anglicized with chaotic results. The reforms introduced are so successful that the army is no longer needed, illness vanishes and crime disappears. Consequently soldiers, doctors and lawyers find themselves out of jobs. To restore the proper balance government by party is introduced. "In ev'ry mental lore" is sung by two scheming Utopian judges, Scaphio and Phantis. "Society has quite forsaken all her wicked courses" is delivered by King Paramount and the Flowers of Progress when the unwitting monarch is persuaded to conduct a court reception in the manner of a minstrel show.

The Grand Duke

This, the final collaboration between Gilbert and Sullivan, was a failure, and subsequent amateur revivals have failed to revise that judgment of the work. The opera involves a theatrical troupe in the Grand Duchy of Pfennig Halbpfennig in 1750. The group is in conspiracy against the penny-pinching Grand Duke Rudolph. They manage to assume rule of the duchy for one night. Things do not work out as they expected, however, and they are all relieved when Rudolph manages to regain his position. "So ends my dream" is sung by Julia Jellicoe, an English comedienne working with the troupe, when she seems to have lost her fiancé and a chance to share the ducal throne.

"Little maid of Arcadee"

Lit..tle maid of Ar..ca..dee, Sat by Cou..sin Ro..bin's knee,

Thought in face and form and limb No....bo...dy could e...qual him.

He was rich and she was fair, Truth they made a pret..ty pair,

Ra....pid....ly e...nough; until Af..ter, say, a month or two,

Robin did as Robins do — Fickle as the month of May,

Jilted her and ran a....way, Wretched lit..tle mai..den she,

Dole..ful maid of Ar...ca..dee. Dole..ful maid of Ar...ca......dee,

"When first my old, old love I knew"

tank,   Tink a tank,   tink a tank,   tink a tank,   I   used   to   mope,   and

Tink a tank,   Tink a tank,   Tink,   tink a tank,   tink a

sigh,   and   pant,   Just like a   love - s'ck   boy.

tank,   tink a tank,   Tink,   tink,   tink,   Tink a tank.

But

"When I, good friends, was call'd to the bar"

beauti - ful blue, A brief which I bought of a boo - - by, A couple of shirts and a

collar or two, And a ring that looked like a ru - - - by. He'd a couple of shirts and a

collar or two, And a ring that look'd like a ru - by.

2. In Westminster Hall I danced a dance,
    Like a semi-despondent fury;
For I thought I never should hit on a chance
    Of addressing a British jury.
But I soon got tired of third-class journeys,
    And dinners of bread and water ;
So I fell in love with a rich attorney's
    Elderly, ugly daughter.
       Chorus—So he fell in love, &c.

3. The rich attorney he jumped with joy,
    And replied to my fond professions :
" You shall reap the reward of your pluck, my boy,
    At the Bailey and Middlesex Sessions.
You'll soon get used to her looks," said he,
    " And a very nice girl you'll find her !
She may very well pass for forty-three
    In the dusk, with a light behind her !"
       Chorus—She has often been taken for forty-three, &c.

4. The rich attorney was good as his word,
    The briefs came trooping gaily,
And every day my voice was heard
    At the Sessions or Ancient Bailey.
All thieves, who could my fees afford,
    Relied on my orations,
And many a burglar I've restored
    To his friends and his relations.
       Chorus—And many a burglar he's restored, &c.

For 5th Verse turn over.

"When I, good friends, was call'd to the bar"   9

"With a sense of deep emotion"

of a heart-less wile, See the trait-or, all de-fi-ant, Wear a su-per-ci-lious

dolce.   CHORUS. *Unis.*

smile, Sweet-ly smil'd my cli-ent on him, Coy-ly woo'd and gent-ly won him. Sweet-ly smil'd his cli-ent

on him, Coy-ly woo'd and gent-ly won him.

COUNSEL. (*With increased energy.*)   *cres.*

Swift-ly fled each hon-eyed hour, Spent with this un-man-ly male, Cam-ber-well be-came a bow'r,

CHORUS. *Unis.*

Peckham, an Ar-cad-ian vale, Breath-ing con-cen-tra-ted ot-to, An ex-is-tence *a la Watteau.* Bless us

"O gentlemen, listen I pray"

1. O gen-tle-men, lis-ten I
2. can-not eat breakfast all

ALLEGRETTO NON TROPPO VIVACE.

pray, Tho' I own that my heart has been rang-ing, Of na-ture the laws I o-
day; Nor is it the act of a sin-ner, When break-fast is ta-ken a-

-bey, For na-ture is con-stant-ly chang-ing: The moon in her pha-ses is
-way, To turn his at-ten-tion to din-ner; And it's not in the range of be-

found, The time, and the wind, and the wea-ther, The months in suc-ces-sion come
-lief, To look up-on him as a glut-ton, Who, when he is tir-ed of

round, And you dont find two Mon - days to - ge - ther. Ah! . . . con - si - der the mo - ral, I
beef, De - ter - mines to tac - kle the mut - ton. Ah! . . . but this I am will - ing to

pray, Nor bring a young fel - low to sor - row, Who loves this young la - dy to - day, And loves that young
say, If it will ap - pease her sor - row, I'll mar - ry this la - dy to - day, And I'll mar - ry the

CHORUS—BRIDESMAIDS.

la - dy to - mor-row! Con - si - der the mor - al, we pray, Nor bring a young fel - low to
o - ther to - mor-row! But this he is will - ing to say, If it will ap - pease her

sor - row, Who loves this young la - dy to - day, And loves that young la - dy to - mor-row! You
sor - row, He'll mar - ry this la - dy to - day, And he'll mar - ry the o - ther to - mor-row!

first time. SOLO.

last time.

- mor-row!

"Time was, when Love and I"

head-ache? sigh'd the maids as-sem-bled; Had I a cold? well'd forth the silent tear; Did I look pale? then

half a pa-rish trem-bled; And when I cough'd all thought the end was near! I had no care— no jealous doubts hung

o'er me, For I was lov'd beyond all o-ther men. Fled gild-ed dukes and belt-ed earls be-fore me, Ah

me, ah me, I was a pale young cu-rate then! A pale young cu-rate, a pale young

cu-rate, Ah me, I was a pale young cu-rate then!

Ped. * Ped. *

cres. f colla voce.

"Welcome joy! adieu to sadness!"

faction in a-pos-tro-phe like this: San-ga-zure im-mor-tal, San-ga-zure di-vine!

Wel-come to my por-tal, An-gel, oh be mine! Im-mor-tal, di-vine! An-gel, oh be mine!

Ir-re-sis-ti-ble in-cen-tive Bids me hum-bly kiss your hand; I'm your ser-vant most at-

-ten-tive, Most o-be-dient to com-mand!

LADY S.

Sir, I thank you most po-lite-ly For your grace-ful cour-te-see; Com-pli-ment more tru-ly

knight-ly Ne-ver yet was paid to me! Chi-val-ry is an in-gre-dient Sad-ly lack-ing in our

land— Sir, I am your most o-be-dient, Most o-be-dient to com-mand. Wild with a-do-ra-tion! Mad with fas-ci-

na-tion! To in-dulge my la-men-ta-tion No oc-ca-sion do I miss! Goad-ed to dis-trac-tion By madden-ing in-

-ac-tion, I find some sa-tis-fac-tion In a-pos-tro-phe like this: Mar-ma-duke im-mor-tal,

Mar-ma-duke di-vine; Take me to thy por-tal, Loved one, oh be mine! Im-

-mor - tal, di - vine! Loved one, oh be mine! .. Chi - val - - ry is

SIR. M.

Wild with a - do - ra - tion! Mad with fas - ci -

an in - - gre - - dient Sad - ly .. lack - - ing

- na - tion! To in - dulge my la - men - ta - tion No oc - ca - sion do I miss! Wild with a - do - ra - tion! To in -

in .. our .. land. Wild with a - do - ra - tion! Mad with fas - ci -

- dulge my la - men - ta - tion No oc - ca - sion do I miss! I'm .. your .. ser - vant

na - tion! To indulge my la - men - ta - tion No oc - ca - sion do I miss! To in - dulge my la - men -

most at - ten - tive, Most o - be - dient

"My name is John Wellington Wells"

name is John Wellington Wells, . . . I'm a deal-er in ma-gic and spells, . . . In bless-ings and cur-ses, And

e - ver-fill'd pur - ses, In pro-phe - cies, wit-ches, and knells. . . If you want a proud foe to "make tracks"— . . If you'd

melt a rich un-cle in wax—. . . . You've but to look in On the re-si-dent Djinn, Number sev-en-ty, Sim-me-ry

Axe. . . . We've a first rate as-sortment of ma-gic; And for rais-ing a posthumous shade, With ef-

-fects that are co-mic or tra-gic, There's no cheap-er house in the trade. . . . Love-phil-tre, we've quan-ti-ties

of it! And for know-ledge if a-ny one burns, . . . We're keep-ing a ve-ry small pro-phet, a pro-phet Who

brings us unbound-ed re-turns: . . For he can pro-phe-sy With a wink *of* his eye, Peep with se-cu-ri-ty

In - to fu - tu - ri - ty, Sum up your his - to - ry, Clear up a mys - te - ry, Hu - mour pro - cli - vi - ty

For a na - ti - vi - ty, for a na - ti - vi - ty; He has answers o - ra - cu - lar, Bo - gies spec - ta - cu - lar,

Te - tra - pods tra - gi - cal, Mir - rors so ma - gi - cal, Facts as - tro - no - mi - cal, So - lemn or co - mi - cal,

And, if you want it, he Makes a re - duc - tion on ta - king a quan - ti - ty! Oh! . . . . If

cre - - scen - - do.

a - ny - one a - ny - thing lacks, . . He'll find it all rea - dy in stacks, . . If he'll on - ly look in On the

re - si - dent Djinn, Num-ber se - ven-ty, Sim - me - ry Axe!

He can raise you hosts Of ghosts, And that, with - out re - flec - tors; And

cree - py things With wings, And gaunt and gris - ly spec - tres; He can fill you crowds Of

shrouds, And hor - ri - fy you vast - ly; He can rack your brains With chains, . . And

gib - ber - ings grim and ghast - ly! Then, if you plan it, he Chan-ges or - ga - ni - ty, With an ur - ba - ni - ty

Full of sa - ta - ni - ty, Vex - es hu - ma - ni - ty With an in - a - ni - ty Fa - tal to va - ni - ty,

Driv - ing your foes to the verge of in - sa - ni - ty! Bar - ring tau - to - lo - gy, In de - mon - o - lo - gy,

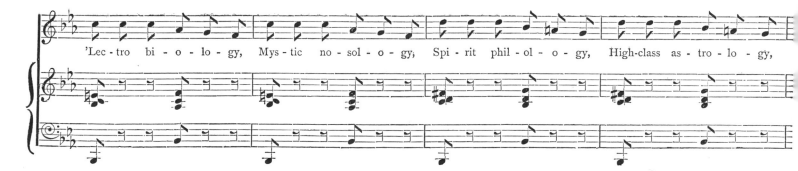

'Lec - tro bi - o - lo - gy, Mys - tic no - sol - o - gy; Spi - rit phil - ol - o - gy, High-class as - tro - lo - gy,

Such is his know-ledge, he Is - n't the man to re - quire an a - po - lo - gy! Oh! . . . . My

name is John Wel - ling - ton Wells, . . I'm a deal - er in ma - gic and spells, . . . In bless-ings and cur - ses, And

e - ver-fill'd pur - ses, In pro - phe - cies, witch - es, and knells. . . And if a - ny - one a - ny-thing lacks, . . . He'll

cres. *molto.*

find it all rea - dy in stacks, . . If he'll on - ly look in On the re - si - dent Djinn, Number se-ven - ty, Simmer - y

Axe

ff

"Dear friends, take pity on my lot"

bad - ly.

_f_ CHORUS.

You ve-ry plain old man, she loves you mad - - ly!

Moderato à la Valse.

I know not why I love him so; It

is en - chant - ment, sure - ly! He's dry and snuf - fy, deaf and slow, Ill-

Oh! You're ev'-ry-thing that I de-test, But still I love you dear - ly! You're all that I de - test, I love you

dear - - - - ly! . . . I caught that line, but for the rest I did not hear it clear - ly!

f You

ve - ry plain old man, She loves you mad - - ly!

"We sail the ocean blue"

"I'm called little Buttercup"

I've trea-cle and tof-fee, I've tea and I've cof-fee, Soft tom-my and suc-cu-lent chops;

I've chick-ens and co-nies, And pret-ty po-lo-nies, And ex-cel-lent pe-per-mint drops. . . .

. . . Then buy of your But-ter-cup, Dear lit-tle But-ter-cup, Sail-ors should ne-ver be shy—

So buy of your But-ter-cup, Poor lit-tle But-ter-cup, Come, of your But-ter-cup buy.

"A maiden fair to see"

A mai-den fair to see, The pearl of min-strel-sy; A bud of blush-ing beau-ty For whom proud no-bles sigh, And with each o-ther vie, To do her me-nial's duty. To do her me-nial's du-ty. A sui-tor low-ly born, With hope-less pas-sion torn, And poor be-yond con-ceal-ing— Hath dar'd for her to pine, At whose ex-al-ted shrine A world of wealth is kneel-ing. A world of wealth is kneel-ing. Un-learn-ed he in aught Save that which love hath taught, For

"I am the captain of 'Pinafore'"

very, very good, And, be it un-der-stood, He com-mands a right good crew.
-ceed-ing-ly po-lite, And he thinks it on-ly right To re-turn the com-pli-ment.

Tho' re -
Bad

-la-ted to a peer, I can hand, reef, and steer, Or ship a sel-va-gee; I am
lan-guage or a-buse I ne-ver, ne-ver use, What e-ver the e-mer-gen-cy; Though

ne-ver known to quail At the fu-ry of a gale, And I'm ne-ver, ne-ver sick at
"both-er it" I may. . . . Oc-ca-sion-al-ly say, I ne-ver use a big, big

"I am the monarch of the sea"

an-chor here I ride, My bo-som swells with pride, And I snap my fin-gers at a

foe-man's taunts. And so do his sis-ters and his cou-sins and his aunts.

Cousin Hebe.

Sopranos.
And so do his sis-ters and his

Tenors & Basses.
And so do his sis-ters and his

His sis-ters and his cou-sins and his aunts.

cou-sins and his aunts, His sis-ters and his cou-sins and his aunts.

cou-sins and his aunts, His sis-ters and his cou-sins and his aunts.

Sir J. Porter.
But

when the breez-es blow I gen-e-ral-ly go be-low, And seek the se-clu-sion that a

"When I was a lad"

now I am the ru-ler of the Queen's Na-vee.

He po-lished up that han-dle so care-ful-lee That
He co-pied all the let-ters in a hand so free, And

He po-lished up that han-dle so care-ful-lee That
He co-pied all the let-ters in a hand so free, And

now he is the ru-ler of the Queen's Na - vee.

now he is the ru-ler of the Queen's Na - vee.

3. In serving writs I made such a name
   That an articled clerk I soon became ;
   I wore clean collars and a bran new suit
   For the pass examination at the Institute.
    And that pass examination did so well for me,
    That now I am the ruler of the Queen's Navee.

     CHORUS.—And that pass examination, &c.

4. Of legal knowledge I acquired such a grip
   That they took me into the partnership,
   And that junior partnership I ween
   Was the only ship that I ever had seen.
    But that kind of ship so suited me,
    That now I am the ruler of the Queen's Navee.

     CHORUS.—But that kind, &c.

5. I grew so rich that I was sent
   By a pocket borough into Parliament.
   I always voted at my party's call,
   And I never thought of thinking for myself at all.
    I thought so little they rewarded me,
    By making me the ruler of the Queen's Navee.

     CHORUS.—He thought so little, &c.

6. Now landsmen all, whoever you may be,
   If you want to rise to the top of the tree,
   If your soul isn't fettered to an office stool,
   Be careful to be guided by this golden rule, —
    Stick close to your desks and never go to sea,
    And you all may be rulers of the Queen's Navee.

     CHORUS.—Stick close, &c.

"Never mind the why and wherefore"

"He is an Englishman!"

"Oh, better far to live and die"

pi - rates all are well-to-do, But I'll be true to the song I sing, And live and die a
wants to call his crown his own, Must man - age some - how to get through More dir - ty work than

cresc.   *rall.*

a tempo.

Pi - rate King, } For .. I am a Pi - rate King ! . . . . . . And it
ever I do. }

p

is, it is a glo - rious thing to be a Pi - rate King ! . . . . For I am a Pi - rate

King . . . . .   And it is, it is a glo - rious thing to

CHORUS. *f*

You are ! Hur - rah for the Pi - rate King ! . .

f   *p*

"Poor wand'ring one"

CHORUS OF GIRLS.

Take heart, no dan-ger lowers; Take a - ny heart but ours.

MABEL.

Take heart, fair days will shine; Take a - ny heart— take mine!

CHORUS.

Take heart, no dan-ger lowers; Take . . a - ny heart but ours.

MABEL.

Take heart, fair days will shine; Take a - ny heart— take mine! Ah! . . . .

Ah! . . . . . . Ah! . . . . Ah! . . . .

cre - - - scen - - - do. . .

Poor wan - - d'ring one, ... Though thou hast sure - ly stray'd.

Take heart of grace, Thy steps re - trace, Poor . . . wan - - d'ring

one! Ah, ah! . . Ah, ah, ah!

CHORUS.

Poor wan - - d'ring one! Poor wan - - d'ring

Ah, ah! . . . Ah, ah, ah! Fair days will shine, Take . . . .

one! Take heart, Take

8va.

"I am the very model of a modern Major-General"

quote the fights his - to - ri - cal, From Ma - ra - thon to Wa - ter - loo, in or - der ca - te - go - ri - cal. I'm
crimes of He - lio - ga - ba - lus! In co - nics I can floor pe - cu - li - a - ri - ties pa - ra - bo - lous. I can

ve - ry well ac - quaint - ed, too, with mat - ters ma - the - ma - ti - cal; I un - der - stand e - qua - tions, both the
tell un - doubt - ed Ra - pha - els from Ge - rard Dows and Zoff - an - ies. I know the croak - ing cho - rus from the

sim - ple and quad - ra - ti - cal: A - bout bi - no - mial The - o - rem I'm teem - ing with a lot o' news,
"Frogs' of A - ris - to - pha - nes! Then I can hum a fugue, of which I've heard the mu - sic's din a - fore,

(*Dialogue.*)

1. With ma - ny cheer - ful facts a - bout the square of the hy - po - ten - use;
2. And whis - tle all the airs from that in - fer - nal non - sense, *Pin - a - fore!*

64   *The Pirates of Penzance*

be - ings a - ni - mal - cu - lous. In short, in mat - ters ve - ge - ta - ble, a - ni - mal, and mi - ne - ral, I

- rac - ta - cus - 's u - ni - form. In short, in mat - ters ve - ge - ta - ble, a - ni - mal, and mi - ne - ral, I

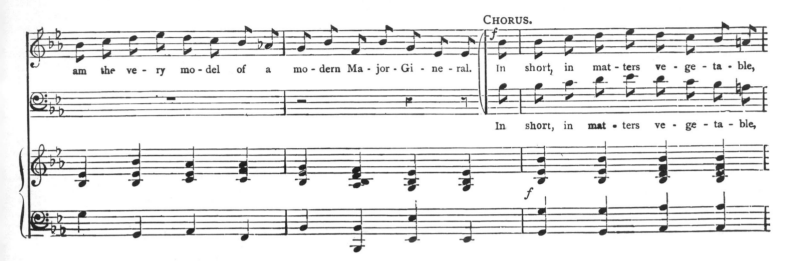

CHORUS.

am the ve - ry mo - del of a mo - dern Ma - jor - Gi - ne - ral. In short, in mat - ters ve - ge - ta - ble,

In short, in mat - ters ve - ge - ta - ble,

a - ni - mal, and mi - ne - ral, He is the ve - ry mo - del of a mo - dern Ma - jor - Gi - ne - ral!

a - ni - mal, and mi - ne - ral, He is the ve - ry mo - del of a mo - dern Ma - jor - Gi - ne - ral!

3. In fact, when I know what is meant by "ma - me - lon" and "ra - ve - lin;" When

Slower.

-gin-ning of the cen-tu-ry, But still, in mat-ters ve-ge-ta-ble, a-ni-mal, and mi-ne-ral, I

CHORUS.

am the ve-ry mo-del of a mo-dern Ma-jor-Ge-ne-ral. But still, in mat-ters ve-ge-ta-ble,

But still, in mat-ters ve-ge-ta-ble,

a-ni-mal, and mi-ne-ral, He is the ve-ry mo-del of a mo-dern Ma-jor-Ge-ne-ral.

a-ni-mal, and mi-ne-ral, He is the ve-ry mo-del of a mo-dern Ma-jor-Gi-ne-ral.

"When the foeman bares his steel"

The Pirates of Penzance

Go . . . and do your best . . en-dea - vour And, . . . be-fore all links we se - - ver,

We . . . will say fare - - well . . for e - ver. Go to glo - ry and the grave!

cre - - - - - scen - - - do . . . .

CHORUS OF GIRLS.

Go to glo - ry and the grave! For your foes are fierce and ruth - less, False, un -

8va.

f   *fz*

- mer - ci - ful, and truth - less; Young and ten - der, old and tooth - less, All in vain their mer - cy crave!

8va.

F

p

"When you had left our pirate fold"

ge-nious pa-ra-dox! We've quips and quib-bles heard in flocks, But none to beat this pa-ra-dox

ge-nious pa-ra-dox! We've quips and quib-bles heard in flocks, But none to beat this pa-ra-dox!

1st & 2nd verse.

A pa-ra-dox, a pa-ra-dox, a most in-ge-nious pa-ra-dox. Ha, ha, ha, ha, ha, ha, ha, ha, this

FRED. **1st & 2nd verse.**

A pa-ra-dox, a pa-ra-dox, a most in-ge-nious pa-ra-dox. Ha, ha, ha, ha, ha, ha, ha, ha, a

1st & 2nd verse.

A pa-ra-dox, a pa-ra-dox, a most in-ge-nious pa-ra-dox. Ha, ha, ha, ha, ha, ha, ha, ha, this

2. this

pa - ra - dox.

pa - ra - dox.

pa - ra - dox.

We

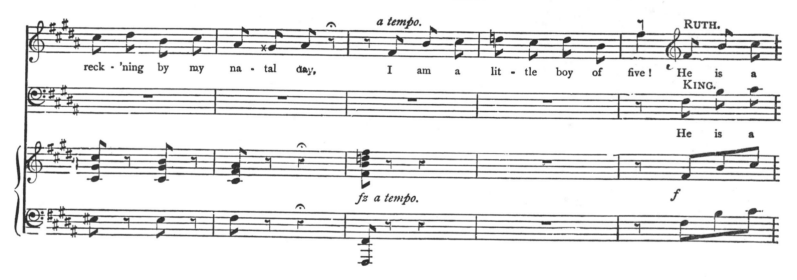

"When a felon's not engaged in his employment"

"With cat-like tread"

Come, friends, who plough the sea, Truce to na - vi - ga - tion, Take an - o - ther sta - tion;

Ra, ra, ra, ra, ra, ra, ra, ra, ra, ra, ra, ra, ra, ra, ra, ra,

Let's va - ry pi - ra - cee With a lit - tle bur - gla - ree! Come, friends, who

ra, ra, ra, ra, ra, ra, ra, ra, ra, ra, ra, ra, ra! Ra, ra, ra, ra,

plough the sea, Truce to na - vi - ga - tion, Take an - o - ther sta - tion; Let's va - ry pi - ra - cee..

ra, ra, ra, ra, ra, ra, ra, ra, ra, ra, ra, ra, ra, ra, ra, ra, ra, ra, ra,

cre - scen - - do. .

SOLO. SAMUEL.

With a lit - tle bur - gla - ree! Here's your crow - bar, And . . your . .

ra, Ta-ran - ta - ra, ra, ra

"I cannot tell what this love may be"

eyes so ___ won _ drous red? Though ev _ ery _

_ where true love I see A - com _ ing to

all, _ but not to me, I can _ not tell what _ this love _ may be! _

_ For I _ am blithe and I _ am gay, While they _ sit sigh _ ing night and

day; For I— am blithe and I— am gay, Think of the gulf 'twixt them— and

CHORUS. *f*

Yes, she is blithe and she is gay, Yes, she is

me, Think of the gulf 'twixt them and me, Fal la la la

blithe and gay, Yes, she is blithe and gay.

la la la la la la la la la la la la la la la la la la la la, and mi _ se _ rie!

Ah, mi _ se _ rie!

sigh? Though ev - 'ry - where true love I

see A-com-ing to all,— but not to

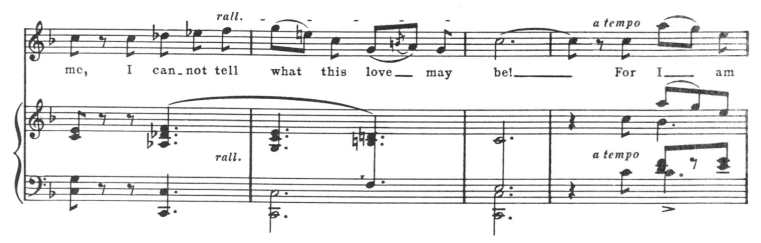

me, I can-not tell what this love— may be!——— For I— am

blithe and I— am gay, While they— sit sigh - ing night— and

"If you want a receipt"

pluck of Lord Nel _ son on board of the Vic _ to _ ry— Ge _ nius of Bis _ mark de
want a re _ ceipt for this sol _ dier _ like pa _ ra _ gon, Get at the wealth of the

_ vis _ ing a plan— The hu _ mour of Field _ ing,(which sounds con _ tra _ dic _ to _ ry)—
Czar (if you can)— The fam _ i _ ly pride of a Span _ iard from Ar _ ra _ gon—

Cool _ ness of Pa _ get a _ bout to tre _ pan— The sci _ ence of Jul _ lien, the
Force of Me _ phis _ to pro _ nounc _ ing a ban— A smack of Lord Wa _ ter _ ford,

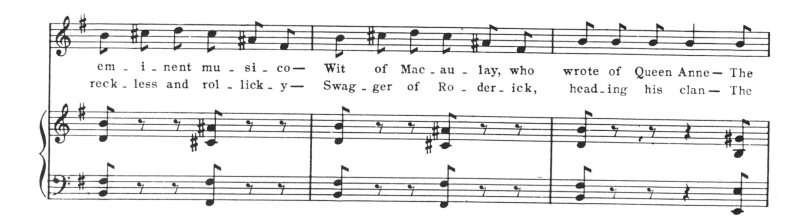

em _ i _ nent mu _ si _ co— Wit of Mac _ au _ lay, who wrote of Queen Anne— The
reck _ less and rol _ lick _ y— Swag _ ger of Ro _ der _ ick, head _ ing his clan— The

pa_thos of Pad_dy, as ren_dered by Bou_ci_cault— Style of the Bish_op of
keen pen_e_tra_tion of Pad_ding_ton Pol_la_ky— Grace of an O_da_lisque

So_dor and Man— The dash of a D'Or_say, di_vest_ed of quack_e_ry—
on a di_van— The ge_nius stra_te_gic of Cæ_sar or Han_i_bal—

Nar_ra_tive pow_ers of Dick_ens and Thac_ke_ray— Vic_tor Em_man_u_el—
Skill of Sir Gar_net in thrash_ing a can_ni_bal— Fla_vour of Ham_let— the

peak-haunt_ing Pe_ve_ril— Tho_mas A_qui_nas, and Doc_tor Sa_che_ve_rell—
Strang_er, a touch of him— Lit_tle of Man_fred (but not ve_ry much of him)—

Tup _ per and Ten _ ny _ son _ Dan _ iel De _ foe _ An _ tho _ ny Trol _ lope and
Bea _ dle of Bur _ ling _ ton _ Ri _ chard _ son's show _ Mis _ ter Mi _ caw _ ber and

cres _ _ _ _ cen _ _ do

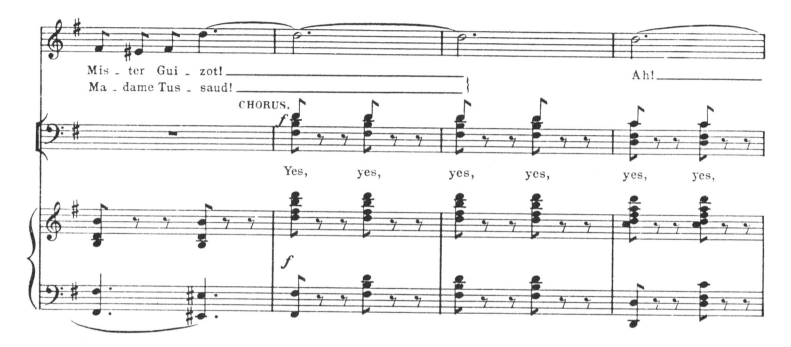

Mis _ ter Gui _ zot! _____ Ah! _____
Ma _ dame Tus _ saud! _____

CHORUS.

Yes, yes, yes, yes, yes, yes,

Take of these el _ e _ ments all that is fu _ si _ ble,

yes, yes! A Hea _ vy Dra _ goon, a Hea _ vy Dra _ goon, a

Melt them all down in a pip_kin or cru_ci_ble, Set them to sim_mer and take off the scum,___

Hea_vy Dragoon, a Hea_vy Dragoon, a Hea_vy Dragoon, a Hea_vy Dragoon___

2nd time

___ And a Hea___vy Dra_goon is the re___si_du___um!

is the re___si_du___um!

f   *ff*

1.   **2.**

2. If you

ff

"Am I alone, And unobserved?"

-vere   Is but a   mere   Ve _ neer!   This cy_nic

smile   Is but a   wile   Of guile!   This cos_tume

chaste   Is but good taste   Mis _ placed!

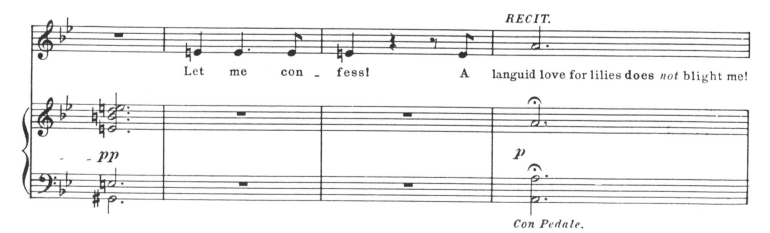

RECIT.

Let   me   con _ fess!   A   languid love for lilies does *not* blight me!

Con Pedale.

Lank limbs and haggard cheeks do *not* delight me! I do *not* care for dirty greens By any means. I do

not long for all one sees That's Japanese.—I am *not* fond of uttering platitudes In stained-glass attitudes.

In short, my me-di-æ-val-is-m's af-fec-ta-tion. Born of a

mor-bid love of ad-mi-ra-tion!

Allegretto grazioso. (♩=72.)

p

1. If you're

anx_ious for to shine_in the high æs_the_tic line_ as a man of cul ture
el_o_quent in praise of the ve_ry dull old days which have long since passed a_
sen_ti_men_tal passion of a ve_ge_ta_ble fash_ion must ex_cite your lan_guid

rare, You must get up all the germs of the trans_cen_den_tal terms, and_ plant them ev_ery_
_way, And con_vince 'em, if you can, that the reign of good Queen Anne was Cul_ture's palmiest
spleen, An at_tachment *à la* Plato for a bash_ful young po_ta_to, or a not-too-French French

_where. You must lie up_on the daisies and dis_course in nov_el phrases of your compli_ca_ted state of
day. Of___ course you will pooh-pooh what_ev_er's fresh and new, and de_clare it's crude and
bean! Though the Phil_is_tines may jostle, you will rank as an a_pos_tle in the high æs_the_tic

mind, The meaning doesn't mat_ter if it's on_ly i_dle chat_ter of a trans_cen_den_tal
mean, For Art stopped short in the cul_ti_va_ted court of the Em_press Jo_seph_
band, If you walk down Pic_ca_dil_ly with a pop_py or a lil_ly in your me_di_æ_val

kind.   And   ev_er_y_one will   say,   As you walk your mys_tic
_ine.   And   ev_er_y_one will   say,   As you walk your mys_tic
hand.   And   ev_er_y_one will   say,   As you walk your flow_ery

pp sempre stacc.

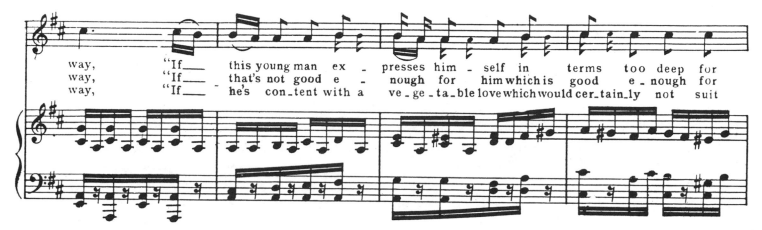

way,   "If__   this young man ex_presses him_self in   terms   too deep for
way,   "If__   that's not good e_nough for himwhichis   good   e_nough for
way,   "If__   he's con_tent with a   ve_ge_ta_ble lovewhichwould cer_tain_ly not suit

me,   Why,   what a ve_ry sin_gu_lar_ly   deep young man this deepyoung man must
me,   Why,   what a ve_ry cul_ti_va_ted   kind of youth this kind of youth must
me,   Why,   what a most par_tic_u_lar_ly   pure youngman this pure youngman must

last verse rall.

bel"
bel"
bel"

1. 2.   **3.**

2. Be__
3. Then a

"Prithee, pretty maiden"

(Hey, but he's dole_ful, willow willow wa_ly!) No_bo_dy I care for comes a-courting me—

Hey wil_low wa_ly O! No_bo_dy I care for Comes a-courting—there_fore,

rall. GROSVENOR. *a tempo*

Hey__ wil__ low wa_ly_ O! Prithee, pret_ty mai_den, will you mar_ry me?

(Hey, but I'm hope_ful, wil_low wil_low wa_ly!) I may say, at once, I'm a

man of pro_per_tee— Hey wil_low wa_ly O! Mo_ney, I des_pise it;

Many people prize it, Hey — wil — low wa — ly — O! Gentle sir, al-though to

mar-ry I de-sign— (Hey, but he's hope-ful, wil-low wil-low wa — ly!) As

yet I do not know you, and so I must de-cline, Hey wil-low wa — ly O! To

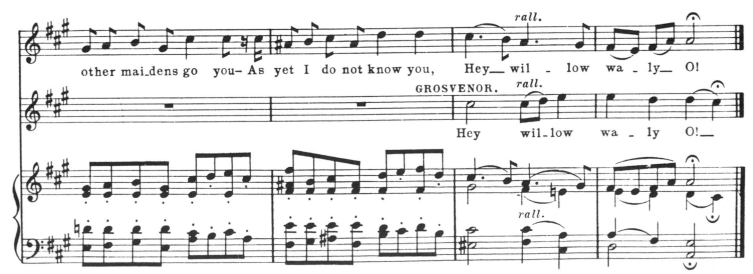

other mai-dens go you— As yet I do not know you, Hey — wil — low wa — ly — O!

Hey wil-low wa — ly O!—

"Sad is that woman's lot"

life's un_cer_tain gloamings,   To wreathe her wrinkled brow with well-saved

"combings;"   Re_duced, with rouge,   lip-salve,   and pear_ly grey,

To "make up" for lost   time   as best she may!

Andante moderato. ♩ = 80.

Silvered is the   ra _ ven hair, Spreading is the   part_ing straight,

Mottled the com_plex_ion fair, Halt_ing is the_youth_ful gait, Hol_low is the laughter free,

Spec _ ta _ cled the lim _ pid eye— Lit _ tle will be left_ of_ me In the

com _ ing by and bye! Lit _ tle will be left of me In the com _ ing by and

bye!

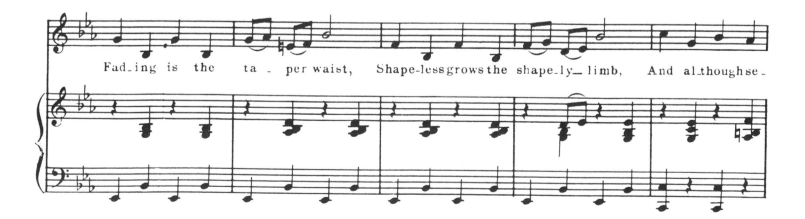

Fad _ ing is the ta _ per waist, Shape-less grows the shape _ ly _ limb, And although se-

-vere-ly-laced, Spreading is the_ fi _gure trim! Stout_er than I used to be,

Still more cor_pu_lent grow I—— There will be too much_ of_ me In the

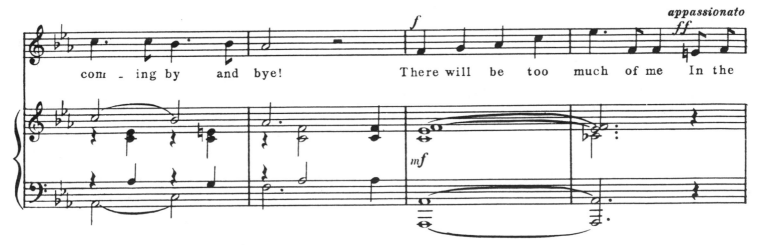

com_ing by and bye! There will be too much of me In the

com_ing_by and bye!

"A magnet hung in a hardware shop"

felt no whim, Though he charm-ed i-ron,it

charmed not him, From nee-dles and nails and knives he'd turn, For he'd set his love

CHORUS OF MAIDENS.   GROSVENOR.

on a Sil-ver Churn!   A   Sil-ver Churn?   A

Sil-ver Churn!   His-most æs-the-tic. Ve-ry mag-ne-tic

Fan-cy took this-turn—   "If   I can whee-dle A knife or a nee-dle,

The kettles they boiled with rage, 'tis said,

While ev_ery nail went off its head, And

hi_ther and thi_ther be _ gan to roam, Till a hammer came up _

cres _ cen _ do _

_ and drove them home.

CHORUS OF MAIDENS.

It drove them home?

GROSVENOR.

It drove them home! While this mag _ ne _ tic,_

118   *Patience*

Pe_ri_pa_te_tic_ Lov_er he lived to_ learn, By no en_dea_vour Can

mag_net e_ver At_tract a Sil_ver Churn!

CHORUS OF MAIDENS.

While this mag_ne_tic,_

CHORUS AND GROSVENOR.

Pe_ri_pa_te_tic_ Lov_er he lived to_ learn, By no en_dea_vour Can

rall.

mag_net e_ver Attract a Sil_ver Churn!

a tempo

rall.

ff

"So go to him"

"When I go out of door"

fun than "Mon _ day Pops." Who's fond of his din _ ner, And doesn't get thinner On

GROSVENOR.

bot _ tled beer and chops. A com _ mon _ place young man, A

BUNTHORNE.

A com _ mon _ place young man, A

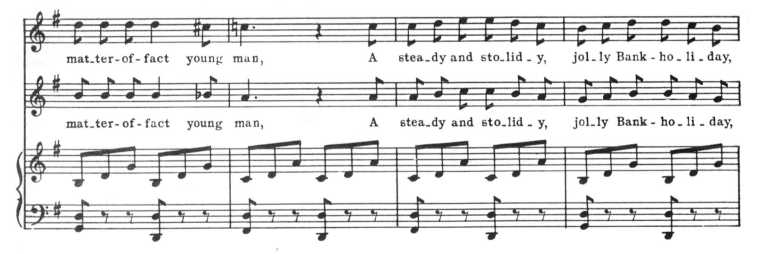

mat _ ter - of - fact young man, A stea _ dy and sto _ lid _ y, jol _ ly Bank - ho _ li _ day,

mat _ ter - of - fact young man, A stea _ dy and sto _ lid _ y, jol _ ly Bank - ho _ li _ day,

Ev _ e _ ry - day young man!

Ev _ e _ ry - day young man! A Ja _ pa _ nese young man, A

blue - and-white young man, Fran _ ces_ca di Ri _mi _ ni, mi_mi_ ny, pim_ i _ ny,

GROSVENOR.

Je _ ne_sais_quoi young man! A Chan_ce_ry Lane young man, A

Som_er_set House young man, A ve_ry de_lec_ta_ble, high_ly re_spec_ta_ble

BUNTHORNE.

Three-pen_ny-bus young man! A pal_lid and thin young man, A

haggard and lank young man, A green-er-y - yal-ler-y, Gros-ve-nor Gallery,

GROSVENOR.

Foot-in-the-grave young man! A Sew-ell and Cross young man, A

How-ell and James young man, A push-ing young par-ti-cle —what's the next ar-ti-cle—

GROSVENOR.

Wa-ter-loo House young man! Conceive me, if you can, A mat-ter-of-fact young

BUNTHORNE.

Conceive me, if you can, A crotch-e-ty cracked young

man,   An al‿pha‿be‿ti‿cal, a‿rith‿me‿ti‿cal, Ev‿e‿ry day young man!   Con‿

man,   An ul‿tra po‿e‿ti‿cal, super-æs‿the‿ti‿cal, Out-of-the-way young man!   Con‿

‿ceive me, if   you   can,   A mat‿ter-of-fact   young man,   An

‿ceive me, if   you   can,   A crotch‿e‿ty, cracked young man,   An

al‿pha‿be‿ti‿cal, a‿rith‿me‿ti‿cal, Ev‿e‿ry-day young man!

ul‿tra po‿e‿ti‿cal, super-æs‿the‿ti‿cal, out-of-the-way young man!

"Tripping hither, tripping thither"

sing, Round a - bout our fai - ry ring.

sing, Round a - bout our fai - ry ring.

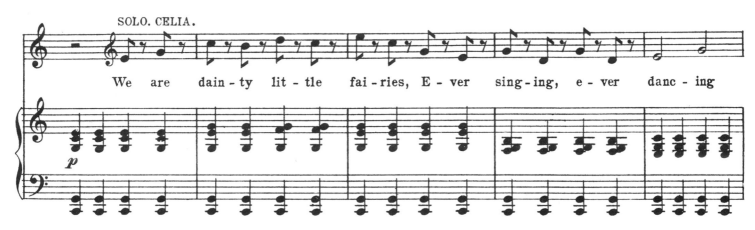

SOLO. CELIA.

We are dain - ty lit - tle fai - ries, E - ver sing - ing, e - ver danc - ing

We in - dulge in our va - ga - ries In a fash - ion most en - tranc - ing.

stacc.

If you ask the spe - cial func - tion Of our ne - ver ceas - ing mo - tion, We re -

-ply with some com - punc - tion That we have - n't a - ny no - tion,

CHORUS.

No, we haven't a - ny no - tion! a - ny no - tion!   Tripping hither, tripping

No, we haven't a - ny no - tion! a - ny no - tion!   Tripping hither, tripping

thither, No - bo - dy knows why or whither, We   must dance and we must sing,   Round a -

thither, No - bo - dy knows why or whither, We   must dance and we must sing,   Round a -

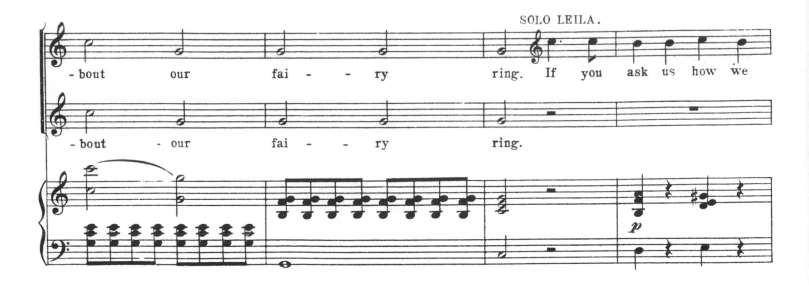

SOLO LEILA.

-bout our fai - - ry ring. If you ask us how we

-bout - our fai - ry ring.

live, Lov - ers all es - sen - tials give; We can ride on

lov - ers' sighs, Warm our - selves in lov - ers'- eyes, Bathe our - selves in

lov - ers' tears, Clothe our - selves with lov - ers' fears,

Arm our-selves with lov-ers' darts, Hide our-selves in lov-ers' hearts,

When you know us you'll dis-co-ver That we al-most live on

lov-er. Yes, we live on lov-er. Tripping hi-ther, tripping

Yes, we live on lov-er. Tripping hi-ther, tripping

thi-ther, No-bo-dy knows why or whi-ther, We must dance and we must

thi-ther, No-bo-dy knows why or whi-ther, We must dance and we must

sing, Round a - bout our fai - ry ring.

sing, Round a - bout our fai - ry ring.

We are dain - ty lit - tle fai - ries, E - ver sing - ing, e - ver

We are dain - ty lit - tle fai - ries, E - ver sing - ing, e - ver

danc - ing, We in - dulge in our va - ga - ries In a

danc - ing, We in - dulge in our va - ga - ries In a

"Loudly let the trumpet bray" (March of the Peers)

trades-men, bow, ye mass-es, Blow the trum-pets, bang the brass-es, Tan-tan-ta-ra! Tzing,

boom!

Bow, bow, ye low-er mid-dle class-es, Bow, bow, ye

trades-men, bow, ye mass-es, Blow the trum-pets, bang the brass-es.

Tan - tan-ta-ra, tan-ta - ra, tan-ta-ra, tan-ta - ra, tan-ta-ra! Tzing, boom, tzing, boom!

Tzing, boom, tzing, boom!   Tzing, boom, tzing, boom!

cresc.   *ff*

legato

We are___ Peers of___ high - est___ sta - tion,

p

Pa - ra - gons of___ le - gis - la - tion,

Pil - lars__ of the__ Bri - tish__ na - tion.

Tan - tan-ta-ra, tan - ta - ra, Tzing, boom, tzing, boom, tan-ta-ra, Tzing, boom!

We are__ Peers of__ high - -est__

We are Peers of high - est sta - tion, Pa - ra - gons of

sta - - tion, Pa - - - ra - gons of____

le - gis - la - tion, Pil - lars of the Bri - tish na - tion,

le - - gis - - la - - tion, Pil - - lars____

Pil - lars of the Bri - tish na - tion, We are Peers of

of the____ Bri - - tish____ na - - tion.____

high - est sta - tion, Pa - ra - gons of le - gis - la - tion.

-ra, tan-tan-ta-ra, tan-ta-ra, tan-ta-ra, tan-ta-ra, tan-ta-ra, ra, ra, ra,

-ra, tan-tan-ta-ra, tan-ta-ra, tan-ta-ra, tan-ta-ra, tan-ta-ra, ra, ra, ra,

ra!   Tan - ta - ra!   Tan - ta - ra! _____

ra!   Tan - ta - ra!   Tan - ta - ra! _____

152   *Iolanthe*

"The Law is the true embodiment"

Chan - ce - ry, All ve - ry a-gree-a-ble girls— and none Are o - ver the age of

twen - ty-one. A plea-sant oc - cu - pa - tion for A

CHORUS OF PEERS.

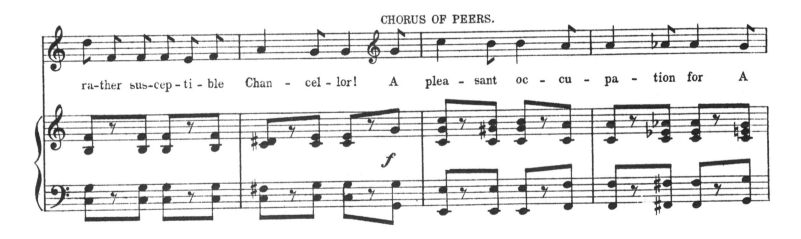

ra-ther sus-cep-ti - ble Chan - cel - lor! A plea - sant oc - cu - pa - tion for A

ra-ther sus-cep-ti - ble Chan-cel - lor!

2. But

154 *Iolanthe*

though the com - pli - ment im - plied In - flates me with le - gi - ti-mate pride, It

nev - er - the - less can't be de - nied, That it has its in - con - ve - ni - ent side.

For I'm not so old, and not so plain, And I'm

quite pre - pared to mar - ry a - gain, But there'd be the deuce to pay in the Lords If I

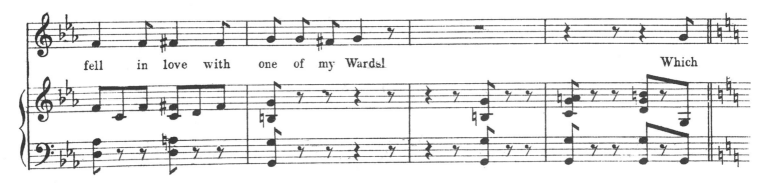

fell in love with one of my Wards! Which

ra - ther tries my tem - per, for I'm *such* a sus-cep-ti-ble Chan - cel - lor! Which

ra - ther tries his tem - per, for He's *such* a sus-cep-ti-ble Chan - cel - lor!

3. And ev - 'ry - one who'd

mar - ry a Ward Must come to me for my ac-cord, And in my court I

sit all day Giv-ing a-gree-a - ble girls a - way,

With

156　*Iolanthe*

one for him— and one for he— And one for you— and one for ye— And

one for thou— and one for thee— But nev-er, oh nev-er a one for me!

Which is ex-as-per-a-ting, for A high-ly sus-cep-ti-ble

CHORUS OF PEERS.

Chan - cel - lor! Which is ex-as-per-a-ting, for A high-ly sus-cep-ti-ble

Chan - cel - lor!

"Spurn not the nobly born"

LORD TOLLOLER.

Spurn not the no-bly born, With love_ af - fect - ed! Nor treat with vir-tuous scorn The

well con-nect-ed! High rank in-volves no shame, We boast an e - qual claim With him of hum-ble name To

be res-pect-ed! Blue blood, blue blood! When vir-tuous love is sought, Thy

pow'r is_ naught, Though dat-ing from the Flood, Blue blood,_ ah. blue blood!

CHORUS. TENORS.

When

BASSES.

When

vir-tuous love is sought, Thy pow'r is _ naught, Though dat-ing from the Flood, Blue blood ah, blue blood!

vir-tuous love is sought, Thy pow'r is _ naught, Though dat-ing from the Flood, Blue blood, blue blood!

LORD TOL.

Spare us the bit-ter pain Of stern de - ni -als, Nor with low born dis-dain Aug - ment our tri-als;

p

cresc. molto

Hearts just as pure and fair May beat in Bel-grave Square As in the low-ly air Of

f

cresc. molto

f

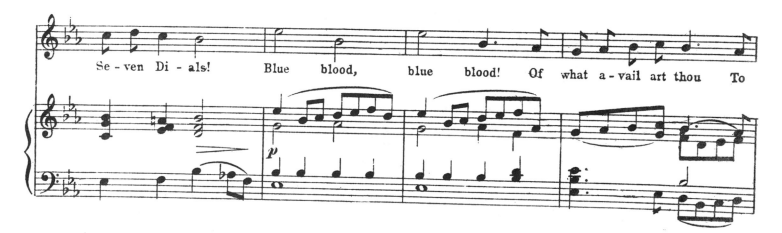

Se - ven Di - als! Blue blood, blue blood! Of what a-vail art thou To

p

"When I went to the Bar"

never as-sume that a rogue or a thief Is a gen-tle-man wor-thy im-
learn-ed pro-fes-sion I'll nev-er dis-grace By tak-ing a fee with a

-pli-cit be-lief, Be - cause his at-tor-ney has sent me a brief, (Said
grin on my face, When I have-n't been there to at - tend to the case, (Said

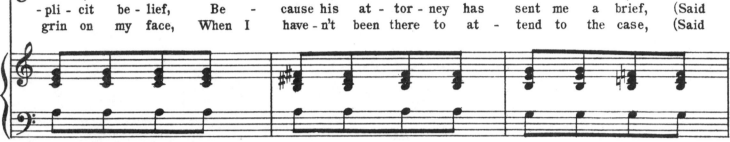

I to my-self— said I!)
I to my-self— said I!)

3. I'll nev - er throw dust in a ju - ry-man's eyes, (Said
4. In o - ther pro - fes-sions in which men en-gage, (Said

I to my-self— said I,) Or hood-wink a judge who is not o-ver-wise, (Said
I to my-self— said I,) The Ar - my, the Na - vy, the Church, and the Stage, (Said

I to my-self— said I,) Or as - sume that the wit-ness-es summoned in force In Ex-
I to my-self— said I,) Pro - fes-sion-al li - cence, if car-ried too far, Your

-che-quer, Queen's Bench, Common Pleas, or Di-vorce, Have perjur'd themselves as a mat-ter of course,)
chance of pro - mo-tion will cer-tain-ly mar— And I fan-cy the rule might ap - ply to the Bar, } (Said

I to my-self— said I!)

2nd time.

"When all night long a chap remains"

1 When all night long a chap re-mains On sen-try-go, to chase mo - no-to-ny He
in that House M. P.'s di - vide, If they've a brain and ce - re - bel-lum, too They've

ex - er - ci - ses of his brains, That is, as-sum-ing that he's got a - ny. Tho'
got to leave that brain out-side, And vote just as their lead-ers tell 'em to. But

nev - er nur-tur'd in the lap Of lux-u - ry, Yet I ad-mon-ish you, I
then the pros-pect of a lot Of dull M. P.'s in close prox - i -mi-ty, All

am an in - tel - lec-tual chap, And think of things that would as - ton-ish you. I
think - ing for them-selves, is what No man can face with e - qua - ni-mi-ty. Then

Tempo I.

of - ten think it's com - i - cal— Fal, lal,— la! Fal, lal,— la! How
let's re - joice with loud Fal lal— Fal, lal,— la! Fal, lal, la! That

Na - ture al - ways does con - trive— Fal lal,— la, la! That— ev - 'ry boy and— ev - 'ry gal That's

born in - to the— world a - live, Is ei - ther a lit - tle Lib - er - al, Or else a lit - tle Con-

- ser - va - tive! Fal, lal,— la! Fal, lal,— la! Is ei - ther a lit - tle Lib - er - al, Or

_mf_

else a lit - tle Con - ser - va - tive! Fal, lal, la!

_ff_

2. When

1. 2.

"When Britain really rul'd the waves"

"Oh, foolish fay"

"Love, unrequited" (Nightmare song)

like,   lies hea - vy on my chest,   And weaves it-self

a tempo

in-to my mid-night slum - bers!

Allegro ma non troppo.

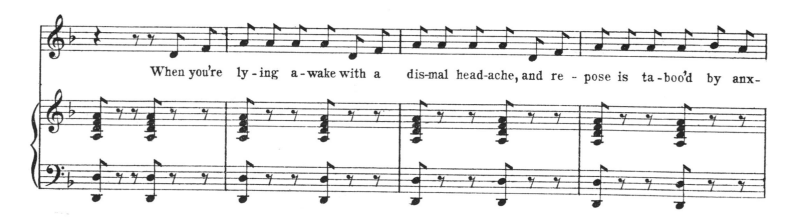

When you're ly - ing a - wake with a   dis-mal head-ache, and re - pose is ta - boo'd by anx-

blank-et-ing tic-kles—you feel like mixed pic-kles—so ter-ri-bly sharp is the

prick-ing, And you're hot, and you're cross, and you tum-ble and toss till there's

no-thing 'twixt you and the tick-ing. Then the bed-clothes all creep to the

ground in a heap, and you pick 'em all up in a tan-gle; Next your pil-low re-signs and po-

-lite-ly de-clines to re-main at its u-su-al an-gle! Well, you

get some re-pose in the form of a doze, with hot eye-balls and head ever-

ach-ing, But your slum-ber-ing teems with such hor-ri-ble dreams that you'd

ve-ry much bet-ter be wak-ing; For you dream you are cross-ing the Channel, and toss-ing a-

-bout in a steam-er from Har-wich Which is some-thing be-tween a large

bath-ing ma-chine and a ve-ry small se-cond class car-riage— And you're

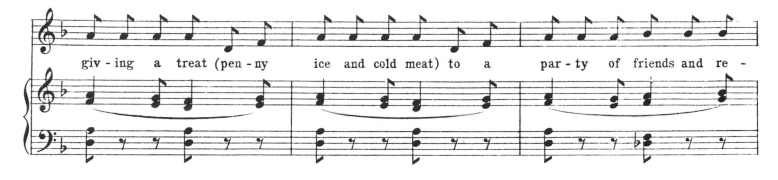

giv-ing a treat (pen-ny ice and cold meat) to a par-ty of friends and re-

-la-tions— They're a ra-ven-ous horde—and they all came on board at Sloane

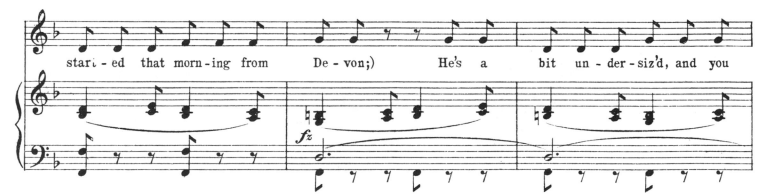

Square and South Kensing-ton Sta-tions. And bound on that jour-ney you find your at-tor-ney (who

start-ed that morn-ing from De-von;) He's a bit un-der-siz'd, and you

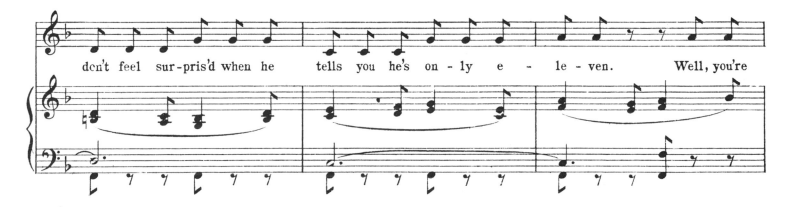

don't feel sur-pris'd when he tells you he's on-ly e-le-ven. Well, you're

driv-ing like mad with this sin-gu-lar lad (by-the-bye the ship's now a four-

-wheel-er,) And you're play-ing round games, and he calls you bad names,when you

tell him that "ties pay the deal-er;" But this you can't stand, so you throw up your hand,and you

find you're as cold as an i-ci-cle; In your shirt and your socks (the black

silk with gold clocks,)cross-ing Sal's-bu-ry Plain on a bi-cy-cle: And

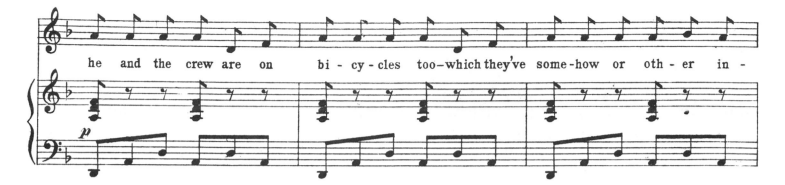

he and the crew are on bi - cy - cles too—which they've some-how or oth - er in -

-vest - ed in— And he's tell - ing the tars, all the par - tic - u - *lars* of a

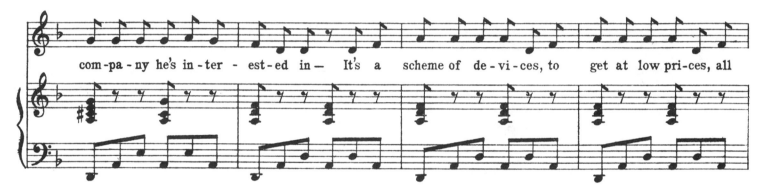

com-pa - ny he's in - ter - est-ed in— It's a scheme of de - vi - ces, to get at low pri-ces, all

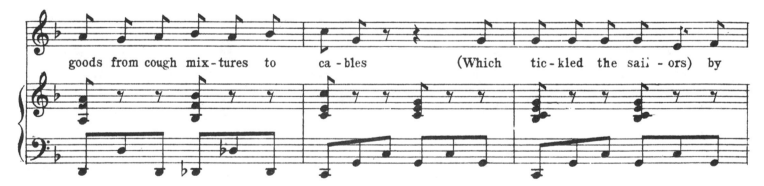

goods from cough mix - tures to ca - bles (Which tic - kled the sail - ors) by

treat - ing re - tail - ers, as though they were all ve - ge - *ta* - bles— You

get a good spades-man to plant a small trades-man, (first take off his boots with a

boot-tree,) And his legs will take root, and his fin - gers will shoot, and they'll

blos-som and bud like a fruit-tree— From the green-gro-cer tree you get grapes and green-pea, cau-li-

-flow - er, pine-ap - ple, and cran-ber-ries, While the pas-try-cook plant, cher-ry

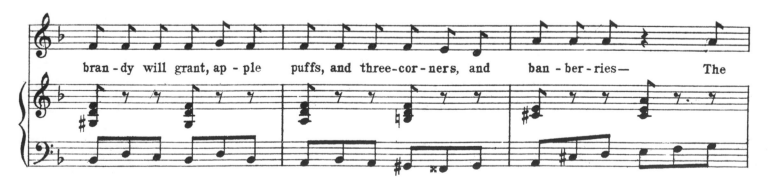

bran-dy will grant, ap - ple puffs, and three-cor-ners, and ban-ber-ries— The

shares are a pen-ny, and e-ver so ma-ny are ta-ken by Roths-child and

Ba-ring, And just as a few are al-lot-ted to you, you a-wake with a shud-der des-

-pair-ing— You're a reg-u-lar wreck, with a crick in your neck, and no

won-der you snore, for your head's on the floor, and you've nee-dles and pins from your

cre -

dark - ness has pass'd, and it's day - light at last, and the night has been

p

long— dit-to, dit-to my song— And thank good-ness they're both of them o -

cre - - scen - - do *f* *colla voce*

- ver!

Con fuoco

ff

"If you go in"

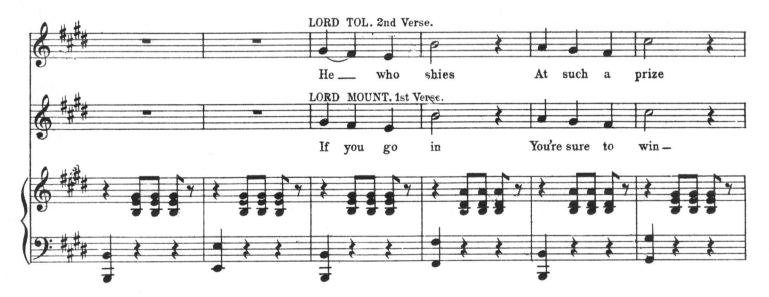

(Together each verse.)

LORD CHAN.

I'll __ take heart, And make a start — Though I fear the

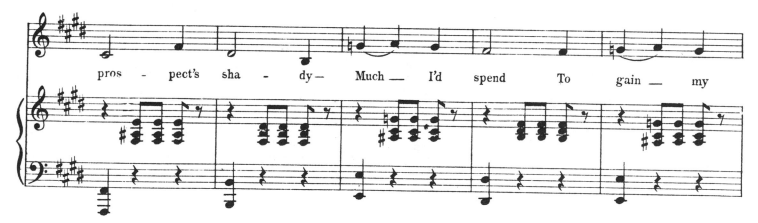

pros - pect's sha - dy— Much __ I'd spend To gain __ my

end — "Faint heart ne - ver won fair la - dy!"

thin— In for a pen - ny, in for a pound— It's.

thin— In for a pen - ny, in for a pound— It's

thin— In for a pen - ny, in for a pound— It's

Love — that makes the world go round! _____

Love — that makes the world go round! _____

Love that makes the world go round! _____

ff

"If you give me your attention"

little plans to snub the self-suf-fi-cient I de-vise; I love my fel-low creatures—I do all the good I can— Yet

ev-'ry bo-dy says I'm such a dis-a-greeable man! And I can't think why!

2. To com-pliments in-fla-ted I've a wi-ther-ing re-ply, And va-ni-ty I al-ways do my

best to mor-ti-fy; A cha-ri-ta-ble ac-tion I can skil-ful-ly dis-sect; And in-ter-est-ed mo-tives I'm de-

-light-ed to de-tect; I know ev-'ry-bo-dy's income and what ev-'ry-bo-dy earns; And I care-ful-ly compare it with the in-come-tax re-turns; But to be-ne-fit hu-man-i-ty how-e-ver much I plan, Yet ev-'ry-bo-dy says I'm such a dis-a-greeable man! And I can't think why!   3. I'm

sure I'm no as-ce-tic; I'm as pleasant as can be; You'll always find me rea-dy with a crushing re-par-tee. I've an

ir - ri - tat - ing chuckle, I've a ce - le - bra - ted sneer, I've an en - ter - tain - ing snig - ger, I've a fas - cin - a - ting leer. To

ev - 'ry - bo - dy's pre - ju - dice I know a thing or two; I can tell a wo - man's age in half a minute—and I do. But al -

- though I try to make my - self as plea - sant as I can, Yet ev - 'ry - bo - dy says I am a dis - a - greeable man! And I

can't think why!
CHORUS. GIRLS.

I can't think why!

He can't think why!
MEN.

He can't think why!

He can't think why!

He can't think why!

"Expressive glances"

Ex-pres-sive glan-ces Shall be our lan-ces, And pops of Sil-le-ry Our light ar-til-le-ry. We'll storm their bow-ers With scent-ed show-ers Of fair-est flow-ers That we can buy!

Chorus. Girls. Oh dain-ty tri-o-let! Oh fra-grant vi-o-let! Oh gen-tle

Men. Oh dain-ty tri-o-let! Oh fra-grant vi-o-let! Oh gen-tle

heigh-o-let (Or lit-tle sigh). On sweet ur-ba-ni-ty, Tho' mere in-a-ni-ty, To touch their va-ni-ty We will re-

heigh-o-let (Or lit-tle sigh). On sweet ur-ba-ni-ty, Tho' mere in-a-ni-ty, To touch their va-ni-ty We will re-

sen - ses With ver- bal fen - ces, With bal-lads a-ma-to-ry And de - cla-ma-to-ry. Lit-tle heed - ing Their pret-ty

plead - ing Our love ex - ceed - ing We'll jus-ti - fy! Our love ex - ceed- ing We'll jus ti - fy! . . .

Chorus. Girls.

. . . Oh dain-ty tri - o - let! Oh fra-grant vi - o - let! Oh gen - tle heigh-o - let! (Or lit - tle sigh). On sweet ur -

Men.

Oh dain-ty tri - o - let! Oh fra-grant vi - o - let! Oh gen - tle heigh-o - let! (Or lit - tle sigh). On sweet ur -

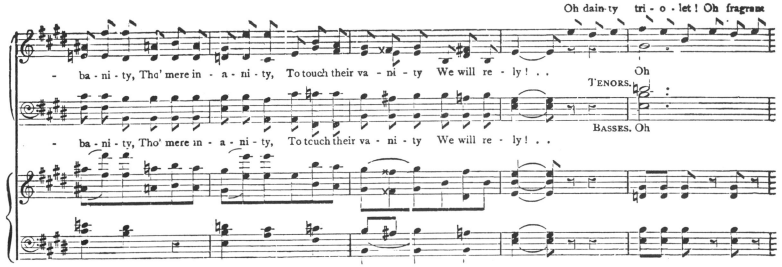

Oh dain-ty tri - o - let! Oh fragrant

- ba - ni - ty, Tho' mere in - a - ni - ty, To touch their va - ni - ty We will re - ly! . .

Tenors. Oh

- ba - ni - ty, Tho' mere in - a - ni - ty, To touch their va - ni - ty We will re - ly! . .

Basses. Oh

"I am a maiden"

So that a maid.. is fair... to see, Ev-'ry maid is the maid for me!

So that a maid is fair to see, Ev-'ry maid is the maid for me!

So that a maid is fair to see, Ev-ry maid is the maid for me!

CYRIL.

2. I am a mai-den frank and sim-ple, Brimming with joy - - ous ... ro-gue-ry;

Mer - ri-ment lurks in ev - 'ry dim - ple, No - bo-dy breaks more hearts than I!

No - bo-dy breaks .... more hearts, more hearts than I! ....

Haugh-ty, hum-ble, coy, or free, Lit-tle care I what maid may be.

Haugh-ty, hum-ble, coy, or free, Lit-tle care I what maid may be.

Haugh-ty, hum-ble, coy, or free, Lit-tle care I what maid may be.

sempre p

So that a maid .. is fair ... to see, Ev-'ry maid is the maid for me!

So that a maid is fair to see, Ev-'ry maid is the maid for me!

So that a maid is fair to see, Ev-'ry maid is the maid for me!

ff   *dim.*

FLORIAN.

3. I am a mai-den coy-ly blush-ing, Ti-mid am I as a star-tled hind;

p

Ev - 'ry suit - or sets me flush - ing, Ev - 'ry suit - or sets me flush - ing

I am the maid . . . that wins man - - kind ! . . .

Haughty, hum - ble, coy, . or free, Lit -tle care I what maid may be.

Haughty, hum - ble, coy, or free, Lit -tle care I what maid may be.

Haughty, hum - ble, coy, or free, Lit -tle care I what maid may be.

So that a maid . . is fair . . to see, Ev - 'ry maid is the maid for me !

So that a maid is fair to see, Ev - 'ry maid is the maid for me !

So that a maid is fair to see, Ev - 'ry maid is the maid for me !

Haugh-ty, hum-ble, coy, or free, Lit-tle care I what maid may be.

Haugh-ty, hum-ble, coy, or free, Lit-tle care I what maid may be.

Haugh-ty, hum-ble, coy, or free, Lit-tle care I what maid may be.

So that a maid is fair to see, Ev-'ry maid is the maid for me! . . . .

So that a maid is fair to see, Ev-'ry maid is the maid for me! . . . .

So that a maid is fair to see, Ev-'ry maid is the maid for me! . . . .

"A Lady fair"

picture of a dis-con-cert - ed Ape.

2. With a view to rise in the

ff *pesante.*

p

so-cial scale, He shav'd his bristles, and he dock'd his tail, . . He grew moustachios, and he took his tub, And he paid a gui-nea to a

toi - let club—And he paid a gui-nea to a toi - let club— But it would not do, The scheme fell through—

p

For the Maid was Beauty's fair-est Queen, With golden tress-es, Like a real prin - cess's, While the Ape, de-spite his

ra - zor keen, Was the A - pi-est Ape that ev- er was seen !

3. He

ff *pesante.*

p

bought white ties, and he bought dress suits, He cramm'd his feet in to bright tight boots—.. And to start in life or a

bran new plan, He christen'd him-self Dar-win-ian Man! He christen'd him-self Dar-win-ian Man! But it

would not do— The scheme fell through, For the Mai-den fair, whom the mon-key crav'd, Was a

ra-diant Be-ing, With a brain far-see-ing—While a Man, how-e-ver well-be-hav'd, At best is on-ly a

mon-key shav'd !   Was a   ra-diant Being,With a brain far-see-ing—While a Man,how-e-ver

HILARION.

For the Maiden fair, whom the monkey crav'd, Was a   ra-diant Being, With a brain far - see-ing—While a Man, how-e-ver

CYRIL.

For the Maiden fair, whom the monkey crav'd, Was a   ra-diant Being, With a brain far - see-ing—While a Man, how-e-ver

FLORIAN.

For the Maiden fair, whom the monkey crav'd, Was a   ra-diant Being, With a brain far - see-ing—While a Man, how-e-ver

well- be-hav'd, At   best is on - ly a   mon - key shav'd !

well- be-hav'd, At   best is on - ly a   mon - key shav'd !

well- be-hav'd, At   best is on - ly a   mon - key shav'd !

well- be-hav'd, At   best is on - ly a   mon - key shav'd !

"Would you know the kind of maid"

CYRIL.

1. Would you know the kind of maid Sets my heart a flame - a?

Eyes must be down - cast and staid, Cheeks must flush for shame - a! She may nei-ther dance nor sing, But, de-mure in

ev 'ry - thing, Hang her head in mo - dest way, With pout - ing lips, . . with pout - ing lips that seem to

say, "Oh kiss me, kiss me, kiss me, kiss me, Though I die of shame - a," Please you, that's the kind of maid

Sets my heart a - flame - a! "Kiss me, kiss me, kiss me, kiss me, Though I die of shame - a," Please you, that's the

kind of maid Sets my heart a flame - a!

2. When a maid is bold and gay, With a tongue goes clang - a, Flaunting it in brave ar - ray, Mai - den may go

hang - a! Sunflow'r gay and hol - ly - hock Ne - ver shall my gar - den stock; Mine the blush - ing rose of May, With

pout - ing lips, . . . with pout - ing lips that seem . . to say, "Oh kiss me, kiss me, kiss me, kiss me,

Though I die of shame - a!" Please you that's the kind of maid Sets my heart a - flame - a! "Kiss me, kiss me,

cres.

kiss me, kiss me, Though I die for shame - a!" Please you that's the kind of maid Sets my heart a -

f

- flame - a!

"Whene'er I spoke"

Ah! . . . . Oh, don't the days seem lank and long When all goes right and nothing goes wrong, And isn't your life ex-

CHORUS.

-tremely flat With nothing whatever to grum-ble at! Oh, isn't your life ex-treme-ly flat With nothing whatever to grum-ble at!

2. When German bands From music stands Play'd Wagner im-per-*fect* - ly—I bade them go—They

didn't say no, But off they went di-rect - ly! The or - gan boys They stopp'd their noise, With

rea - di - ness sur - pris - i.ng, And grin - ning herds Of hur - dy - gurds Re - tired a - po - lo - gis - ing ! Ah! . . . .

. . . . Oh, don't the days seem lank and long When all goes right and nothing goes wrong, And isn't your life ex-tremely flat With

CHORUS.

nothing what-e-ver to grum-ble at ! Oh, isn't your life ex - treme-ly flat With nothing what-e-ver to grum-ble at !

GAMA.

3. I of - fer'd gold In sums un - told To all who'd con - tra - dict me— I

"This helmet, I suppose"

"A wand'ring minstrel I"

On maid-en's cold-ness do you brood? I'll do so too— Oh, ... sor-row, sor-row!

I'll charm your willing ears With songs of lov-er's fears, While sym-pa-the-tic tears my cheeks be-dew—

Allegro marziale.

Oh, ... sor-row, sor-row! But if pa-tri-o-tic sen-ti-ment is

want-ed, I've pa-tri-o-tic bal-lads cut and dried; For wher-e'er our country's ban-ner may be plant-ed, All

o-ther lo-cal ban-ners are de-fied! Our war-ri-ors in ser-ried ranks as-sem-bled, Ne-ver

quail— or they con-ceal it if they do— And I should-n't be surpris'd if na-tions trem-bled Be-fore the migh-ty

troops, the troops of Ti - ti - pu!

MEN. We should-n't be surpris'd if peo - ple trem-bled, trem-bled with a - larm Be - fore the mighty

Allegro pesante, non troppo vivo. (♩ = 160.)

NANKI.
And if you call for a song of the sea, We'll heave the capstan

troops, the troops of Ti - ti - pu!

round, With a yeo heave ho, for the wind is free, Her an-chor's a-trip and her helm's a - lee, Hur - rah for the homeward

MEN. bound! Yeo - ho— heave ho— Hur - rah for the homeward bound!

NANKI.
To lay a - loft in a howl - ing breeze May

tick - le a lands-man's taste, But the hap -piest hour a sail - or sees Is when he's down At an in - land town With his

Nan - cy on his knees, yeo - ho! And his arm a round her waist !

f TENORS.
Then man the cap - stan— off we go, As the

f BASSES.
Then man the cap - stan— off we go, As the

fid - dler swings us round, With a yeo heave ho, And a rum - be - low, Hur - rah for the homeward bound ! . . With a

fid - dler swings us round, With a yeo heave ho, And a rum - be - low, Hur - rah for the homeward bound ! . . With a

Yeo heave ho, ... And a rum - be - low, ... Yeo - ho, heave ho, Yeo -

Yeo heave ho, ... And a rum - be - low, ... Yeo ho, heave ho, . . . Yeo ho, ...

-ho, heave ho, heave ho, heave ho, yeo - ho!

... heave ho, heave ho, heave ho, yeo - ho!

scen - - do. . . . . *ff*

dim.

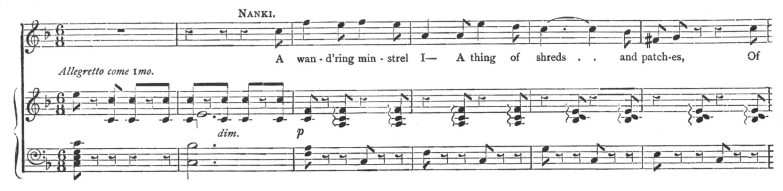

NANKI.

A wan - d'ring min - strel I— A thing of shreds . . and patch-es, Of

Allegretto come 1mo.

dim. *p*

bal - lads, songs and snatch- es, And drea-my lul - la - by, ... And drea-my lul - - -

MEN. *p*

Of

p

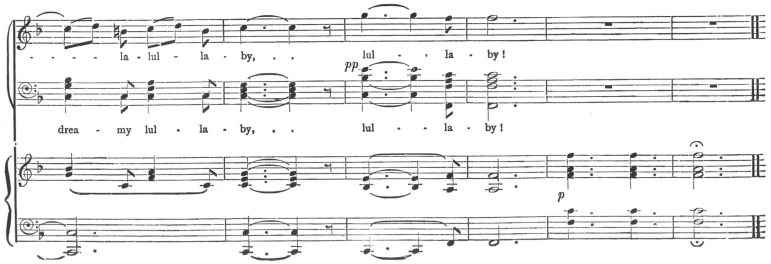

- - - la-lul - la - by, . . lul - la - by!

pp

drea - my lul - la - by, . . lul - la - by!

p

"Behold the Lord High Executioner!"

Ta-ken from the coun-ty jail   By a set of cu-rious chan-ces,   Sure-ly, ne-ver had a

Ta-ken from the coun-ty jail,   Li-ber-a-ted then on bail,   Sure-ly, ne-ver

Ta-ken from the coun-ty jail,   Li-ber-a-ted then on bail,   Sure-ly, ne-ver

male So ad-ven-tur-ous a tale.

had a male So ad-ven-tur-ous a tale.   De - fer, . . . de-fer, . . . To the

had a male So ad-ven-tur-ous a tale.   De - fer, . . . de-fer, . . . To the

Lord High Ex - e - cu-tioner!   De - fer, . . . de-fer, . . . To the

Lord High Ex - e - cu-tioner!   De - fer, . . . de-fer, . . . To the

"As some day it may happen"

some day it may happen that a vic-tim must be found, I've got a lit-tle list— I've got a lit-tle list Of so-ci-e-ty of-fenders who might
nig-ger se-re-nader, and the o-thers of his race, And the pia-no or-gan-ist— I've got him on the list! And the peo-ple who eat peppermint and

well be underground, And who ne-ver would be miss'd—who never would be miss'd! There's the pes-ti-len-tial nui-san-ces who write for au-to-graphs—All
puff it in your face, They ne-ver would be miss'd—They never would be miss'd! Then the i-di-ot who prais-es, with en-thu-si-as-tic tone, All

peo-ple who have flabby hands and ir-ri-tat-ing laughs—All children who are up in dates and floor you with 'em flat— All persons who in shaking hands, shake
cen-tu-ries but this, and ev-'ry country but his own; And the la-dy from the pro-vin-ces, who dress-es like a guy—And "who doesn't think she waltzes, but would

com-pro-mis-ing kind, Such as— what-d'ye call him—Thing'em bob,and like-wise Ne-ver Mind. And 'St—'st—'st— and What s-his-name,and

colla voce.

al-so You-know-who— The task of fill-ing up the blanks I'd ra-ther leave to *you.* But it real-ly does-n't mat-ter whom you

put up-on the list, For they'd none of 'em be missed— they'd none of 'em be missed!

CHORUS OF MEN.

You may put 'em on the list— You may

You may put 'em on the list— You may

f

put 'em on the list; And they'll none of 'em be missed—they'll none of 'em be missed!

put 'em on the list; And they'll none of 'em be missed—they'll none of 'em be missed!

f

"Three little maids"

- thing is a source of fun.

No-body's safe, for we care for none!

Life is a joke that's just be - gun!

Three lit - tle maids from school.   Three lit - tle maids who,

Three lit - tle maids from school.   Three lit - tle maids who,

Three lit - tle maids from school.   Three lit - tle maids who,

"So please you, Sir"

par - don us. So par - don us,

PITTI-SING.

And don't in girl - hood's hap - py spring, Be hard on us, Be hard on us, If

YUM-YUM.

But youth, of course, must

PEEP-BO.

But youth, of course, must

we're designed to dance and sing, Tra la la la la la, But youth, of course, must

CHORUS OF GIRLS.

Tra la la la la la, Tra la la la la la, Tra la la la la la, Tra la la la la

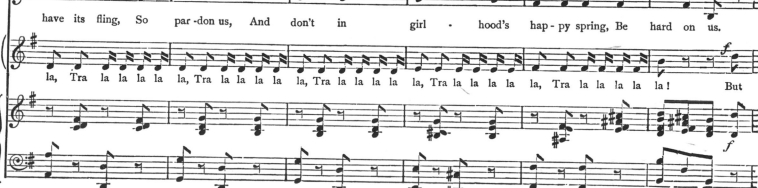

have its fling, So par -don us, And don't in girl - hood's hap - py spring, Be hard on us.

have its fling, So par -don us, And don't in girl - hood's hap - py spring, Be hard on us.

have its fling, So par -don us, And don't in girl - hood's hap - py spring, Be hard on us.

la, Tra la la la la la, Tra la la la la la, Tra la la la la la, Tra la la la la la, Tra la la la la la! But

Tra la la la la la la la la la la la la la la la!

Tra la la la la la la la la la la la la la la la!

Tra la la la la la la la la la la la la la la la!

Tra la la la la la la la la la la la la la la la!

Роон-Ван.

think you ought to re-col-lect You can-not show too much res-pect To-wards the high-ly-ti-tled few; But no-body

Роон-Ван.

Pish-Tush.

does, and why should you? That youth at us should have its fling, Is hard on us, Is hard on us; To

our pre-ro-ga-tive we cling—So par-don us, So par-don us, If we de-cline to dance and

YUM-YUM.
But youth, of course, must have its fling, So par-don us, And

PEEP-BO.
But youth, of course, must have its fling, So par-don us, And

PITTI-SING.
But youth, of course, must have its fling, So par-don us, And

sing, Tra la la la la la, Tra la la la la la, Tra la la la la la, Tra la la la la la, Tra la la la la la, Tra la la la la

Tra la la la la la, Tra la la la la la, Tra la la la la la, Tra la la la la la, Tra la la la la la, Tra la la la la

don't in girl - - hood's hap-py spring, Be hard on us.

don't in girl - - hood's hap-py spring, Be hard on us.

don't in girl - - hood's hap-py spring, Be hard on us.

la, Tra la la la la la, Tra la la la la la, Tra la la la la la la la!

la, Tra la la la la la, Tra la la la la la, Tra la la la la la la la!

CHORUS. f
But youth, of course, must

la la la la la la la!

la la la la la la la!

la la la la la la la!

la la la la la la la!

la la la la la la la!

la la la la la la

"For he's going to marry Yum-Yum"

find   there   are   ma - ny   Who'll wed   for   a   pen - ny,   Who'll wed   for   a   pen -   ny—There are   lots   of   good

fish   in   the   sea !   There are   lots   of good fish   in   the   sea ! There's lots   of good fish,   good fish   in the   sea ! There's lots   of good

fish,   good fish   in the   sea,   in the   sea,   in the   sea,   in the   sea,   in the   sea !

"The sun, whose rays"

real-ly know our worth, The sun and I! Ob-serve his flame, That pla-cid dame, The moon's ce-

-les-tial high-ness; There's not a trace Up-on her face Of dif-fi-dence or shy-ness: She borrows light, That, thro' the night, Mankind may

all ac-claim her, And, truth to tell, She lights up well, So I, for one, don't blame her. Ah,

pray make no mis-take, . . . We are not shy; We're ve-ry wide a-wake! . . . The moon and I!

Ah, pray make no mis-take, We are not shy; We're ve-ry wide a-wake! The moon and I.

"Brightly dawns our wedding day"

"Here's a how-de-do"

laws of com-mon sense We ought-n't to ig - - nore. If what he says is true, 'Tis

laws of com mon sense We ought-n't to ig - nore. If what he says is true, 'Tis

laws of com-mon sense You ought-n't to ig - - nore. If what I say is true, 'Tis

death to mar-ry you! Here's a pret-ty state of things! Here's a pret-ty how-de-do!

death to mar-ry you! Here's a pret-ty state of things! Here's a pret-ty how-de-do!

death to mar-ry you! Here's a pret-ty state of things! Here's a pret-ty how-de-do!

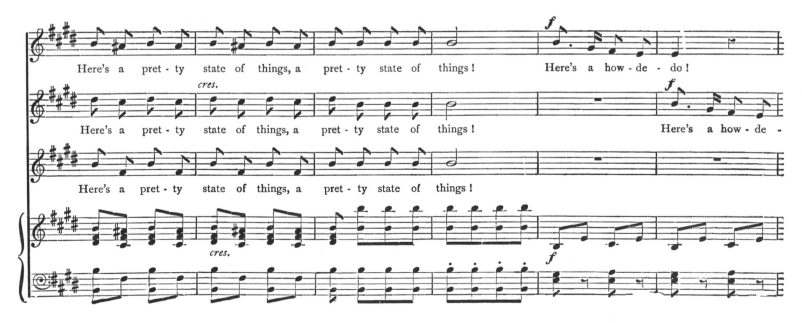

Here's a pret-ty state of things, a pret-ty state of things! Here's a how-de-do!

Here's a pret-ty state of things, a pret-ty state of things! Here's a how-de-

Here's a pret-ty state of things, a pret-ty state of things!

"Miya sama"

Mi - ya sa - ma, mi - ya sa - ma, On - n'm - ma no ma - yé ni Pi - ra - Pi - ra su - ru no wa

Mi - ya sa - ma, mi - ya sa - ma, On - n'm - ma no ma - yé ni Pi - ra - Pi - ra su - ru no wa

Nan . . gia na . . . To - ko ton - ya - ré ton - ya - ré na !

Nan . . gia na . . . To - ko ton - ya - ré ton - ya - ré na !

MIKADO.

From ev - 'ry kind of

daugh-ter-in - law e - lect !

Is

My na -ture is love and light—My free -dom from all . . de · fect—

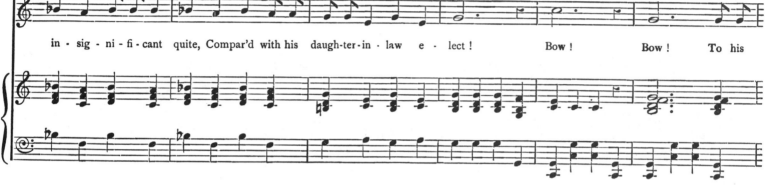

in - sig - ni - fi - cant quite, Compar'd with his daugh-ter-in - law e - lect ! Bow ! Bow ! To his

CHORUS.

daughter -in - law e - lect !

Bow ! Bow ! To his daugh-ter -in - law e - lect !

Bow ! Bow ! To his daugh-ter-in - law e - lect !

dim.

dim.

Attacca

"A more humane Mikado"

work. The la-dy who dyes a che-mi-cal yel-low, Or stains her grey hair puce, Or
Pops. The bil- -liard sharp whom a-ny-one catch-es, His doom's ex-treme-ly hard— He's

pinch-es her fig-ger, Is black'd like a nig-ger With per-ma-nent wal-nut juice. The i-diot who, in
made to dwell—In a dun-geon cell On a spot that's al-ways barr'd. And there he plays ex-

rail-way car-ria-ges, Scribbles on win-dow panes, We on-ly suf-fer To ride on a buf-fer In
-tra-va-gant match-es In fit-less fin-ger stalls, On a cloth un-true With a twist-ed cue, And el-

rall.   *a tempo.*
Par-lia-men-t'ry trains. } My ob-ject all sub-lime I shall a-chieve in time— To
-lip-ti-cal bil-liard balls ! }

let the pun-ish-ment fit the crime—the pun-ish-ment fit the crime ; And make each pris-'ner pent Un-

"The flowers that bloom in the spring"

YUM-YUM.

Tra

PITTI-SING.

Tra

a tempo.

bloom in the spring. Tra la la la la, Tra la la la la, The flow-ers that bloom in the spring. Tra

POOH-BAH.

Tra

la la la la, Tra la la la la, Tra la la la la la!

la la la la, Tra la la la la, Tra la la la la la!

la la la la, Tra la la la la, Tra la la la la la!

la la la la, Tra la la la la, Tra la la la la la!

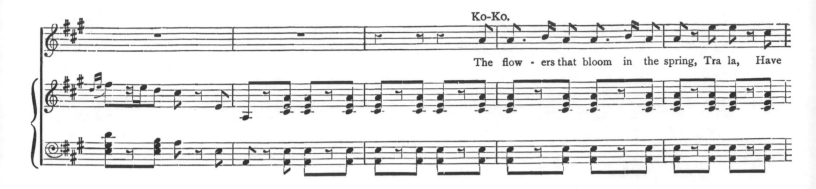

Ko-Ko.

The flow - ers that bloom in the spring, Tra la, Have

no - thing to do with the case. I've got to take un - der my wing, Tra la, A

most un - at - trac - tive old thing, Tra la, With a ca - ri - ca - ture of a face, With a

rall.   *a tempo.*

ca - ri - ca - ture of a face; And that's what I mean when I say, or I sing, "Oh

bo - ther the flow - ers that bloom in the spring, Tra la la la la, . . Tra la la la la, . . Oh

"Alone, and yet alive!"

KATISHA.

A - lone, and yet a - live!

Oh, se - pul-chre! My soul is still my bo - dy's pri - son - er! Re - mote the peace that

Death a - lone can give.— My doom, to wait! my pun-ish-ment, to live!

Hearts do not break! They sting and ache For old love's sake, But do not die!

Though with each breath They long for death, As wit - ness-eth the liv - ing I !— the liv - ing I !

Oh, liv - ing I ! Come, tell me why, When hope is gone Dost

thou stay on ? . . Why lin - ger here, Where all is dear ? Oh, liv - - ing I !

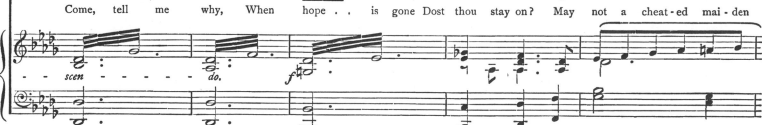

Come, tell me why, When hope . . is gone Dost thou stay on ? May not a cheat - ed mai - den

die ? May not . . a cheat - ed mai - den die ?

"On a tree by a river" (Titwillow)

su - i-cide's grave—"Oh wil-low, tit - wil-low, tit - wil - low!"

3. Now I

feel just as sure as I'm sure that my name Is-n't Wil-low, tit - wil-low, tit - wil-low, That 'twas

blight - ed af - fec - tion that made him ex-claim, "Oh wil-low, tit - wil - low, tit - wil - low!" And if

you re-main cal - lous and ob - du-rate, I Shall per - ish as he did, And you will know why, Though I

pro - bab-ly shall not ex - claim as I die, "Oh wil-low, tit-wil-low, tit - wil-low!"

"There is beauty in the bellow of the blast"

Ko-Ko.
fall - ing of a flight of thun-der - bolts! Yes, in spite of all my meek-ness, If I have a lit - tle weak-ness, It's a

rall. **Both.** *a tempo.*
pas - sion for a flight of thun - der - bolts. It that is so, Sing der - ry down der - ry, It's e - vi - dent, ve - ry, Our

tastes are one. A - way we'll go, And mer - ri - ly mar - ry, Nor tar - di - ly tar - ry, Till day is done!

Ko-Ko.
There is beau - ty in ex - treme old age— Do you

fan - cy you are el - der - ly e - nough? In - for - ma - tion I'm re-quest-ing On a sub-ject in - ter-est - ing: Is

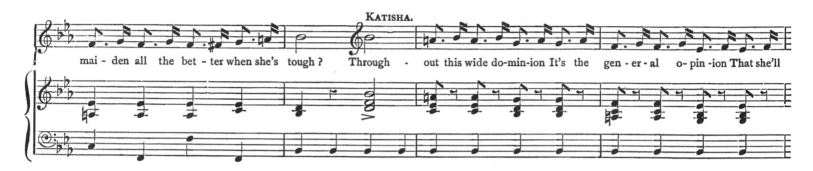

KATISHA.

mai - den all the bet - ter when she's tough? Through - out this wide do-min-ion It's the gen - er - al o - pin-ion That she'll

KO-KO.

last a good deal long - er when she's tough. Are you old e-nough to mar - ry, do you think? Won't you

wait un - til you're eighty in the shade? There's a fas - ci - na-tion fran - tic In a ru - in that's ro-man - tic; Do you

KATISHA.   rall.

think you are suf - fi - ciently de - cayed? To the mat - ter that you men-tion I have gi - ven some at - ten-tion, And I

"If somebody there chanced to be"

"I shipped, d'ye see" and Hornpipe

SOLO. RICHARD.

1. I shipped, d'ye see, in a
'apt'n he up and he
up with our helm, and we

PIANO.

Re-ve-nue sloop, And, off Cape Fi - nis - tere,
says, says he, "That chap we need not fear,—
scuds before the breeze, As we gives a compassion-ating cheer;

A merchantman we see, A Frenchman, go-ing free, So we
We can take her, if we like, She is sar-tin for to strike, For she's
Froggee an-swers with a shout As he sees us go a - bout, Which was

made for the bold Moun - seer, D'ye see? We made for the bold Moun - seer. But she
on - ly a darned Moun - seer, D'ye see? She's on - ly a darned Moun - seer! But to
grate-ful of the poor Moun - seer, D'ye see? Which was grateful of the poor Moun - seer! And I'll

proved to be a Frigate, and she up with her ports, And fires with a thir - ty - two! It come un-common near, But we
fight a French fal-lal— it's like hit-tin' of a gal,—It's a lub-ber-ly thing for to do; For we, with all our faults, Why we're
wa-ger in their joy they kissed each other's cheek, (Which is what them fur-ri-ners do), And they blessed their lucky stars We were

answer'd with a cheer, Which pa-ra-lysed the Par-ley - voo, D'ye see? Which pa-ra lysed the Par-ley - voo! Which
stur-dy Brit-ish salts, While she's on - ly a Par-ley - voo, D'ye see? While she's on - ly a poor Par - ley - voo! While she's
har-dy Brit-ish tars, Who had pi-ty on a poor Par-ley-voo, D'ye see? Who had pi-ty on a poor Par - ley - voo! Who had

SOLO. RICHARD.

pa - ra-lysed the Par - ley-voo, D'ye see? Which pa-ra-lysed the Par-ley-voo! 2. Then our
on - ly a Par - ley-voo, D'ye see? While she's on ly a Par-ley-voo! 3. So we
pi-ty on a Par-ley-voo, D'ye see? Who had pi-ty on a Par - ley - voo!

Attacca Hornpipe.

HORNPIPE.

PIANO.

2nd time melody 8ve. higher.

3 times, I. *f,* II. *pp,* III. *ff.*

"My boy, you may take it from me"

1. My boy, you may take it from me, That of all the af-flic-tions ac-curst With which a man's sad-dled And ham-pered and ad-dled, A dif-fi-dent na-ture's the worst. Though cle-ver as cle-ver can be— A Crichton of ear-ly ro-mance— You must stir it and stump it, And blow your own trum-pet, Or, trust me, you have-n't a chance,

2. Now take, for ex-am-ple, *my* case: I've a bright in-tel-lec-tu-al brain— In all Lon-don ci-ty There's no one so wit-ty—I've thought so a-gain and a-gain. I've a high-ly in-tel-li-gent face— My fea-tures can-not be de-nied— But, what-ev-er I try, sir, I fail in—and why, sir? I'm mod-es-ty per-son-i-fied !

3. As a po-et, I'm ten-der and quaint— I've pas-sion and fer-vour and grace— From O-vid and Ho-race To Swin-burne and Mor-ris, They all of them take a back place. Then I sing and I play and I paint: Though none are ac-complished as I, To say so were trea-son: You ask me the rea-son? I'm dif-fi-dent, mod-est, and shy !

ROBIN.

2nd and 3rd times.

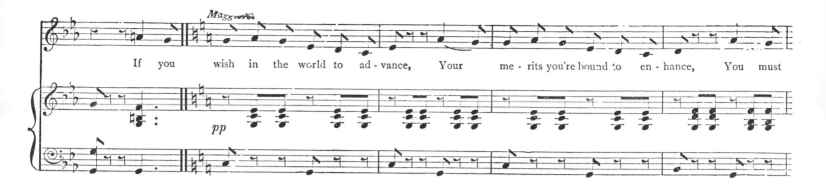

If you wish in the world to ad-vance, Your me-rits you're bound to en-hance, You must

stir it and stump it, And blow your own trum-pet, Or, trust me, you have-n't a chance.

RICHARD.

If you

wish in the world to ad-vance, Your . . me-rits you're bound to en-hance, You must

wish in the world to ad-vance, Your . . me-rits you're bound to en-hance, You must

stir it and stump it, And blow your own trumpet, Or, trust me, you have-n't a chance! chance!

stir it and stump it, And blow your own trumpet, Or, trust me, you have-n't a chance! chance!

"Cheerily carols the lark over the cot"

(*Chuckling.*) He! he! he! Mad, I? Yes, ve-ry! But why? Mys - te-ry! Don't call!

No crime— 'Tis on-ly That I'm love - lone-ly! That's all!

1. To a gar - den full of
2. In a nest of weeds and

po - sies Com - eth one to ga - ther flow - ers, And he wan - ders through its bow - ers Toy - ing
net - tles, Lay a vi - o - let, half - hid - den, Hop - ing that his glance un - bid - den Yet might

"When the night wind howls"

black dogs bay at the moon, Then is the spec - tre's

ho - li - day— then is the ghost's high noon! For

CHORUS. *ff*

Ha ! ha !

Ha ! ha !

then is the ghost's high noon, high noon, ...

Ha ! ha ! high noon, ...

Ha ! ha ! high noon, ...

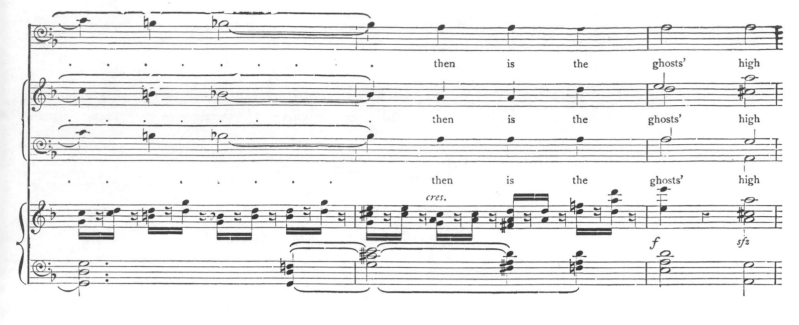

then is the ghosts' high

then is the ghosts' high

then is the ghosts' high

cres.

f   *sfz*

2nd VERSE.

noon !

noon '

noon !

sf   *p*

over the trees   and the mists lie low on the fen,   From

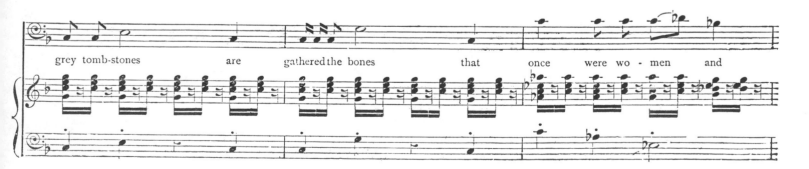

grey tomb-stones   are gathered the bones   that once were wo - men and

men, And a - way they go, with a mop and a mow, to the

re - vel that ends too soon, For cock crow li - mits our

ho - li - day— the dead of the night's high noon! The

CHORUS. *ff*

Ha! ha!

Ha! ha!

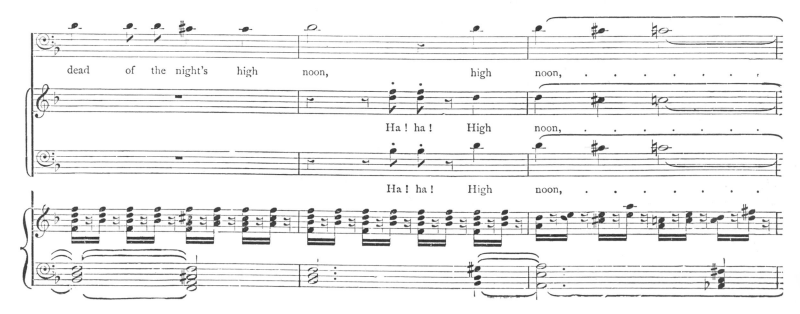

dead of the night's high noon, high noon,

Ha! ha! High noon,

Ha! ha! High noon,

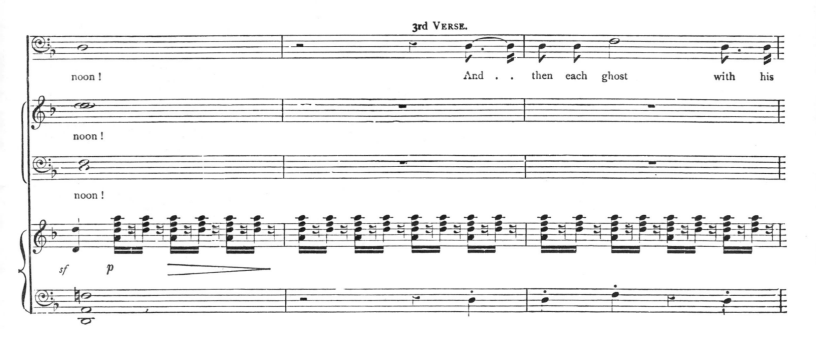

kiss, per - haps, on her lan - tern chaps, and a gris · ly grim, "good

night !" Till the wel - come knell of the mid - night bell rings

forth its jol - li - est tune, And ush ers in our next high

ho - li - day— the dead of the night's high noon ! The

CHORUS. *ff*

Ha ! ha !

Ha ! ha !

"I once was a very abandoned person"

MARGARET.

But be so kind To bear in mind, We were the vic-tims of cir - cum-stan-ces!

That is one of our blame - less dan - ces.

MARGARET. 2nd VERSE.

I was once an ex-ceed-ing-ly odd young la-dy—

SIR DESPARD.

Suf-fer-ing much from spleen and va-pours.

3rd VERSE. SIR DESPARD.　　　　　　　　　　　　　　MARGARET.

I've gi - ven up all my wild proceedings. My taste for a wand-'ring life is wan-ing.

SIR DESPARD.　　　　　　　　　　　MARGARET.　　　　　　　　　　　　SIR DESPARD.

Now I'm a dab at pen - ny read-ings. They are not re-mark - a - bly en - ter-tain - ing.　　A mo - der - ate

　　　　　　　　　　　　　　　　　　　　MARGARET.　　　　　　　　　SIR DESPARD

live - li - hood we're gain-ing.　　In fact we rule A Na - tion - al School. The

du - ties are dull, but I'm not complaining!

This sort of thing takes a deal of train-ing!

"My eyes are fully open"

now to one an-o-ther, Who could give me good ad-vice when he dis-cov-ered I was er-ring, (Which is just the ve-ry fa-vour which on:

you I am con-fer-ring). My ex-is-tence would have made a ra-ther in-ter-est-ing i-dyll, And I might have lived and died a ve-ry

de-cent in-di-widdle. This par-tic-u-lar-ly ra-pid, un-in-tel-li-gi-ble pat-ter Is-n't gen-er-al-ly heard, and if it

If it is it does-n't mat-ter, mat-ter, mat-ter, mat-ter, mat-ter, If it

If it is it does-n't mat-ter, mat-ter, mat-ter, mat-ter, mat-ter, If it is it does-n't mat-ter, mat-ter,

is it does-n't mat-ter!

"When maiden loves"

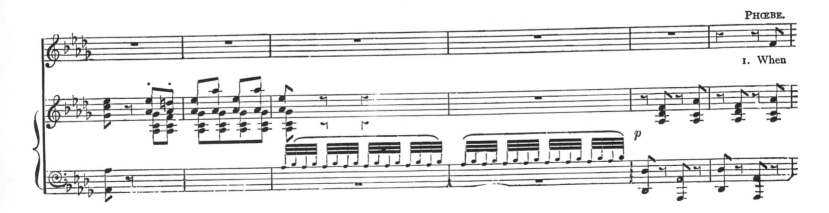

maid - en loves, she sits and sighs, She wan - ders to and fro; Un - bid - den tear- drops fill her eyes, An

to all ques-tions she re - plies, With a sad heigh ho!

'Tis but a lit - tle word— "Heigh-ho! So soft, 'tis scarcely heard— "Heigh-ho!" An i - dle

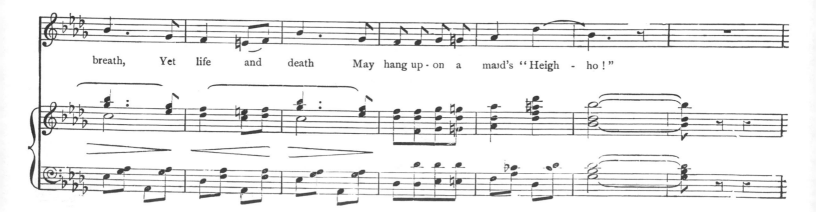

breath, Yet life and death May hang up - on a maid's "Heigh - ho!"

An i - dle breath, Yet life and death May hang up - on a maid's "Heigh - ho!"

2. When

maid - en loves, she mopes a - part, As owl mopes on a tree; Al - though she keen - ly feels the smart, She

can not tell what ails her heart, With its sad "Ah me!"

'Tis but a fool-ish sigh— "Ah me!" Born but to droop and die— "Ah me!" Yet all the

sense Of e - lo - quence Lies hid - den in a maid's "Ah me!"

Yet all the sense Of e - lo-quence Lies hid-den in a maid's "Ah me!" "Ah me!"

"Ah me!" Yet all the sense Of e - lo-quence Lies hid - den

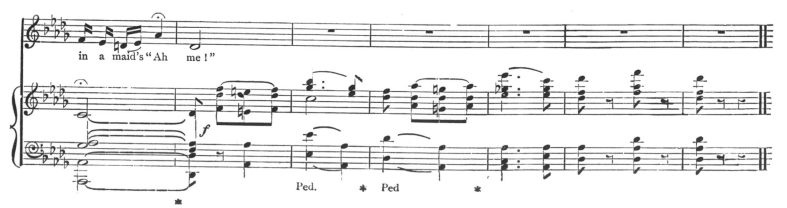

in a maid's "Ah me!"

"Is life a boon?"

kind of plaint have I, Who per ish in Ju ly, Who per ish

in Ju - ly? I might have had to die, . Per -

chance, in June! I might have had to die, . Per - chance, in

June!

2. Is life a thorn? Then count it not a whit Then count it not a whit Nay,

count it not a whit! Man is well done . . with it;

Soon . . as he's born He should all means es say To put the

plague a way; And I, war worn, Poor

cap - tured fu gi tive, My life most glad ly . . . give— I

might have had to live . An - o ther morn ! I

might have had to live, . . . to live An o ther morn !

"I have a song to sing, O!"

PIANO.

POINT.

ELSIE.

I have a song to sing, O! . Sing me your song, O! . . .

POINT.

It is sung to the moon. By a love-lorn loon, Who fled from the mocking throng, O! It's the

song of a mer-ry man, mop-ing mum, Whose soul was sad and whose glance was glum, Who sipped no sup, and who craved no crumb, As he

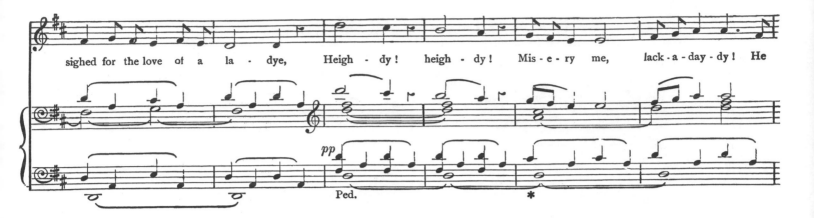

sighed for the love of a la - dye, Heigh - dy! heigh - dy! Mis - e - ry me, lack - a - day - dy! He

sipped no sip, and he craved no crumb, As he sighed for the love of a la - dye!

ELSIE.

POINT.

ELSIE.

I have a song to sing, O! What is your song, O? . . . . It is sung with the ring Of the

songs maids sing Who love with a love life - long, O! It's the song of a mer-ry-maid, peer - ly proud, Who lov'd a lord, and who

312   *The Yeomen of the Guard*

laugh'd a - loud At the moan of a mer-ry-man, mop-ing mum, Whose soul was sore and whose glance was glum, Who sipped no sup, and who

craved no crumb, As he sighed for the love of a la - dye! Heigh - dy! heigh - dy! Mis-e-ry me,

pp

3rd Verse.

lack- a - day - dy ! He sipped no sup, and he crav'd no crumb, As he sighed for the love of a la - dye !

POINT.

ELSIE.

POINT.

I have a song to sing, O ! Sing me your song, O ! . . . . . . It is sung to the knell Of a

crav'd no crumb, As he sighed for the love of a maid ie!   I have a song to sing, O!

POINT.   ELSIE.

Sing me your song, O! . . . .   It is sung with a sigh and a tear in the eye, For it

tells of a right-ed wrong, O! It's a song of a merry maid, once so gay, Who turned on her heel and tripped a - way From the

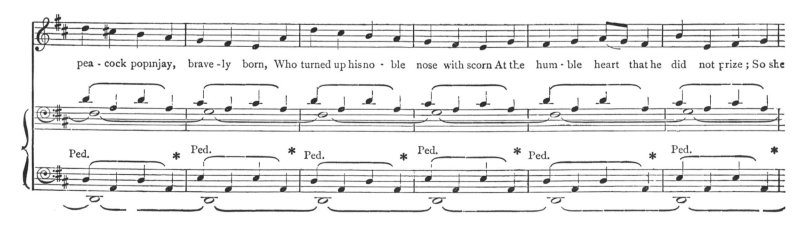

pea - cock popinjay, brave - ly born, Who turned up his no - ble nose with scorn At the hum - ble heart that he did not prize; So she

begged on her knees with down-cast eyes For the love of the mer-ry-man, mo-ping mum, Whose soul was sad and whose

glance was glum, Who sipped no sup. and who craved no crumb, As he sighed for the love of a la-dye!

(Both.)
Heigh-dy! heigh-dy! Mis-e-ry me, lack-a-day-dy! His pains were o'er, and he sighed no more, For he

1st SOPRANOS.
Heigh-dy! heigh-dy! Mis-e-ry me, lack-a-day-dy! His pains were o'er, and he sighed no more, For he

2nd SOPRANOS.
p   *cres.*
Oo . . . .

TENORS & BASSES.   *cres.*
p
Oo . . . .

cres.

molto.

"I've jibe and joke"

"Were I thy bride"

Were I thy bride, Then all the world be - side Were not too wide To hold my wealth of love— Were I thy bride! Up - on thy breast My lo - ving head would rest, As on her nest the ten - der tur - tle dove— Were I thy bride! This heart of mine Would

be one heart with thine, And in that shrine our hap - pi - ness would dwell— Were I thy

bride ! And all day long Our lives should be a song: No grief, no

wrong Should make my heart re - bel— Were I thy bride ! The

sil - v'ry flute, The me - lan - cho - ly lute, Were night owl's hoot To my low - whis - pered coo—

Were I thy bride ! The sky - lark's trill Were

but dis-cord-ance shrill To the soft thrill Of woo-ing as I'd woo—

Were I thy bride! The ro - se's sigh Were

as a car-rion's cry To lul-la-by Such as I'd sing to thee, Were I thy bride!

A fea-ther's press Were lead-en hea-vi-ness To my ca-ress. But then, of

course, you see I'm not thy bride!

"Oh! a private buffoon"

1. Oh! a pri - vate buf - foon is a light-heart - ed loon, If you lis ten to pop - u - lar ru - mour; From the morn to the night he's so joy - ous and bright, And he bub - bles with wit and good hu - mour! He's so quaint and so terse, both in

2. If you wish to suc - ceed as a jes - ter, you'll need To con - si der each per - son's au - ri - cular: What is all right for B would quite scan - da - lize C (For C is so ve - ry par - ti - cular); And D may be dull, and E's

3. If your mas - ter is sur - ly, from get - ting up ear - ly (And tem - pers are short in the morn - ing), An in op - por - tune joke is e - nough to pro - voke Him to give you, at once, a month's warn - ing. Then if you re - frain he is

4. Comes a Bish - op, may be, or a sol - emn D. D.—Oh, be ware of his an - ger pro - vok - ing! Bet - ter not pull his hair—don't stick pins in his chair: He don't un - der - stand prac - ti - cal jok - ing. If the jests that you crack ave an

5. Tho' your head it may rack with a bil - ious at tack, And your sen - ses with tooth-ache you re los - ing, Don't be mo - py and flat—they don't fine you for that, It you're pro - per - ly quaint and a - mus - ing! Tho' your wife ran a - way with a

prose and in verse; Yet though peo - ple for - give his trans - gres - sion,
ve - ry thick skull Is as emp - ty of brains as a la - dle;
at you a - gain, For he likes to get va - lue for mo - ney.
or - tho - dox smack, You may get a bland smile from these sa - ges;
sol - dier that day, And took with her your tri - fle of mo - ney;

There are one or two rules that all
While F is F sharp, and will
He'll ask then and there, with an
But should it, by chance, be im -
Bless your heart, they don't mind—they're ex -

fa - mi - ly fools Must ob - serve, if they love their pro - fes - sion!
cry with a carp, That he's known your best joke from his cra - dle!
in - so - lent stare, "If you know that you're paid to be fun - ny?"
- port - ed from France, Half - a - crown is stopp'd out of your wa - ges!
- ceed - ing ly kind—They don't blame you—as long as you're fun - ny!

There are one or two rules, Half - a -
When your hu - mour they flout, You can't
It adds to the task Of a
It's a gen - e - ral rule, Though your
It's a com - fort to feel If your

do - zen may be, That all fa - mi - ly fools Of what ev - er de - gree,
let your - self go; And it *does* put you out When a per - son says, "Oh,
mer - ry man's place, When your prin - ci - pal asks, With a scowl on his face,
zeal it may quench, If the fa - mi - ly fool Tells a joke that's too French,
part - ner should flit, Tho' *you* suf - fer a deal, They don't mind it a bit—

Must ob - serve, if they love their pro -
I have known that old joke from my
If you know that you're paid to be
Half - a - crown is stopp'd out of his
They don't blame you—so long as you're

1st, 2nd, 3rd, 4th. | **5th.**

fes - sion.
cra - dle!"
fun - ny?
wa - ges!

fun - ny!

"Strange adventure!"

dim
head - ed, In an hour on Tow - er Green!
toll - ing, Toll - ing, toll - ing, Bim - a - boom!
Groom in drea - ry dun geon
Mod - est maid - en will not
head - ed, In an hour on Tow - er Green! Tow - er, Tow - er, Tow - er Green! Groom in drea - ry dun - geon
toll - ing, Toll - ing, toll - ing, Bim - a boom! Bim - a Bim a, Bim a boom! Mod - est maid - en will not
head - ed, In an hour on Tow - er Green! Tow - er. Tow - er, Tow - er Green! Groom in drea - ry dun - geon
toll - ing, Toll - ing, toll - ing, Bim - a - boom! Bim - a, Bim - a, Bim - a - boom! Mod - est maid - en will not
head - ed, In an hour on Tow - er Green!
toll - ing, Toll - ing, toll - ing, Bim - a boom!
Groom in drea - ry dun - geon
Mod - est maid - en will not

cres.
dim.
ly - ing—Groom as good as dead, or dy - ing, For a pret - ty maid - en sigh - ing—Pret - ty maid of sev - en -
tar - ry; Though but six - teen year she car - ry, She must mar - ry, she must mar - ry—Though the al - tar be a

"A man who would woo a fair maid"

of his Jill ! sure . . . of his Jill ! If he wants to make sure of his

Jack, Must stu - dy the knack, But ev 'ry Jack, Must stu - dy the knack If he wants to make sure of his

Jack, Must stu - dy the knack, But ev - 'ry Jack, Must stu - dy the knack If he wants to make sure of his

Jill ! Yes, ev - e - ry Jack, Must stu - dy the knack If he wants . . . to make sure of his

Jill ! Yes, ev e - ry Jack, Must stu - dy the knack If he wants . . . to make sure of his

Jill ! Yes, ev e - ry Jack, Must stu - dy the knack If he wants . . . to make sure of his

Jill !

Jill !

Jill !

"When a wooer Goes a-wooing"

"We're called gondolieri"

"In enterprise of martial kind"

"I stole the Prince"

DON ALHAMBRA.

stole the Prince, and I brought him here And left him, gai - ly pratt - ling With a
sped, and when at the end of a year I sought that in - fant cher - ished, That
owing, I'm much dis - posed to fear, To his terri - ble taste for tip - pling, That
chil - dren followed his old ca - reer— (This state - ment can't be par - ried) Of a

highly re - specta - ble gon - do - lier, Who promised the Roy - al babe to rear, And
highly re - specta - ble gon - do - lier Was lying a corpse on his hum - ble bier— I
highly re - specta - ble gon - do - lier Could never de - clare with a mind sin - cere Which
highly re - specta - ble gon - do - lier: Well, one of the two (who will soon be here)— But

teach him the trade of a ti - mo - neer With his own be - lov - ed brat - ling.
dropp'd a Grand In - qui - si - tor's tear— That gon - do - lier had pe - rished.
of the two was his off - spring dear, And which the Roy - al strip - ling!
which of the two is not quite clear— is the Roy - al Prince you mar - ried!

A
Search

"When a merry maiden marries"

"Then one of us will be a Queen"

that,   With her haugh - ty stare, And her nose in the air, Like a   well-born aris - to - crat!   At ele - gant high so -

ad lib.

colla voce.

- cie - ty talk She'll bear a - way the bell,   With her "How de do?" And her "How are you?" And her "Hope I see you

GIAN. & TESSA.
a tempo.

well!   Oh, . . 'tis a glo - rious thing, I ween, To be a regu - lar Roy - al Queen, No

MARCO & GIUS.
a tempo.

Oh, . . 'tis a glo - rious thing, I ween, To be a regu - lar Roy - al Queen, No

a tempo.

f   dim. p

half-and-half af-fair, I mean, No half-and-half af - fair, But a right down reg-u-lar, reg-u-lar, reg-u-lar,

half-and-half af-fair, I mean, No half-and-half af - fair, But a right down reg-u-lar, reg-u-lar, reg-u-lar,

reg-u-lar Roy - al Queen!

reg-u-lar Roy - al Queen! And no-ble lords will scrape and bow, And dou-ble them in-to two, And

o-pen their eyes In blank sur-prise At what-ev - er she likes to do. And ev-'ry-bo-dy will round-ly vow She's

GIUS.

"Take a pair of sparkling eyes"

ten - der lit - tle hand, Fringed with dain - ty fin - ger - ettes, Press . . . . it, press it—
no - thing more to give. You're a dain - ty man to please,

2nd Verse.

If . . . you're not sat - is-fied,

in pa ren - the - sis ;— Ah ! . . . . . . Take . . . all these, you luck - y
not sa - tis - fied, Ah ! . . . . . Take . . . my coun - sel, hap - py

man— . .Take and keep them, if you can, if you can ! Take all these, you luck - y man, Take and
man ; . .Act up - on it, if you can, if you can ! Take my coun - sel, hap - py man, Act up -

keep . . them, if you can, if . . . you can !
on . . . it, if you can, if . . you can !

Take my coun - sel, hap - py man; Act up - on it, if you

can, if you can, if you can. Act up - on it, if you can, ... hap - py man,

if . . . . you can ! . . . .

"Dance a cachucha"

-nil - la, Mon - te - ro; For wine, when it runs in a - bun-dance, en - han - ces The reck - less de-

-nil - la, Mon - te - ro; For wine, when it runs in a - bun-dance, en - han - ces The reck - less de-

-light of that wild - est of dan - ces, that wild - est of dan - ces, The reck - less de - light! . . . .

-light of that wild - est of dan - ces, that wild - est of dan - ces, The reck - less de - light! . . . .

Dance a ca - chu - cha, fan - dan - go, bo - le - ro, Xe - res we'll drink—Man - za - nil - la, Mon - te - ro—

Dance a ca - chu - cha, fan - dan - go, bo - le - ro, Xe - res we'll drink—Man - za - nil - la, Mon - te - ro—

- light of that wild-est of dan - - - - - - - ces! - - -

- light of that wild-est of dan - - - - - - - ces! - - -

"There lived a King"

-dy, tod - dy. He wished all men as rich as he (And he was rich as rich could be),

MARCO & GIUS.

So to the top of ev - 'ry tree Pro - mo - ted ev - 'ry - bo - dy. Now, that's the kind of King for me— He wished all men as

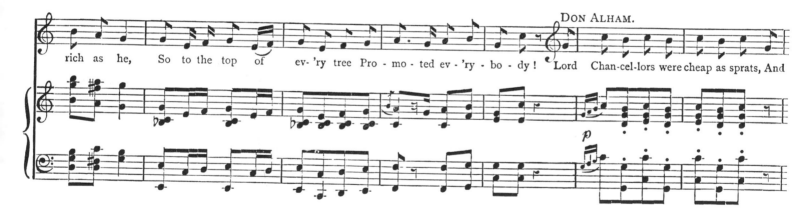

DON ALHAM.

rich as he, So to the top of ev - 'ry tree Pro - mo - ted ev - 'ry - bo - dy ! Lord Chan-cel-lors were cheap as sprats, And

Bish- ops in their sho - vel hats Were plen - ti - ful as tab - by cats— In point of fact, too ma - ny. Am - bas - sa-dors cropped

up like hay, Prime Min - is - ters and such as they Grew like as - pa - ra - gus in May, And Dukes were three a pen - ny. On

ev - 'ry side Field Marshals gleam'd, Small beer were Lords Lieu-ten-ant deem'd, With Ad - mi - rals the ocean teem'd All round his wide do -

- min-ions, With Ad - mi-rals a - round .. his do - min-ions. And Par - ty Lead-ers you might meet In

MARCO & GIUS.

twos and threes in ev - 'ry street Main-tain - ing, with no lit - tle heat, Their va - ri - ous o - pin - ions. Now that's a sight you

could-n't beat—Two Par - ty Lead - ers in each street Main - tain - ing, with no lit - tle heat, Their va - ri - ous o - pin - ions ! That

King, al-though no - one de-nies His heart was of ab - nor-mal size, Yet he'd have act -ed o - ther-wise If he had been a -

- cu - ter. The end is ea - si - ly fore-told, When ev - 'ry bless - ed thing you hold Is made of sil - ver, or of gold, You

long for sim - ple pew-ter. When you have no-thing else to wear But cloth of gold and sat - ins rare, For cloth of gold you

cease to care—Up goes the price of shod-dy, of shod - - - - - - - - - - dy, shod-dy. In

p

short, who-ev-er you may be, To this con-clu-sion you'll a-gree, When ev-e-ry-one is some-bo-dee, Then no one's a-ny-

Marco & Gius.

- bo - dy! Now that's as plain as plain can be, To this con-clu-sion we a-gree—When ev-e-ry-one is

f

some - bo - dee, Then no one's a - ny - bo - dy!

f

"I am a courtier grave and serious"

"In ev'ry mental lore"

spy —to spy Up-on our King's il-li-ci-ties, And keep a watch-ful eye —ful eye On

all his ec-cen-tri-ci-ties. If ev-er a trick he tries, he tries, That sa-vours of ras-

-cal-i-ty, At our de-cree he dies, he dies, With-out the least for-mal-i-ty!

2. We fear no rude re - buff, —re - buff, Or news - pa - per pub -

- li - ci - ty; Our word is quite e - nough, —e - nough, The rest is e - lec - tri - ci - ty. A

pound of dy - na - mite —a - mite Ex - plodes in his au - ri - cu - lars; It's not a plea - sant

sight— sant sight— We'll spare you the par - tic - u - lars. It's force all men con - fess, —con - fess, The

King needs no ad-mon-ish-ing— We may say its suc-cess —suc-cess Is some-thing quite as-

ton-ish-ing. Our des-pot it im-bues, im-bues, With vir-tues quite de-lect-a-ble: He

minds his P's and Q's, and Q's,—And keeps him-self re-spec-ta-ble. Of a tyrant po-lite He's a pa-ra-gon quite. He's as

mod-est and mild In his ways as a child; And no one e'er met With an au-to-crat, yet, So de-light-ful-ly bland To the

least in the land, So de-light-ful-ly bland To the least in the land, So bland,

so bland! O make way for the Wise Men! They are

prize - men— Dou-ble-first in the world's u - ni - ver - si - ty! For though love - ly . . this

is - land (Which is *my* land), She has no one to match them in *her* ci - ty.

"Society has quite forsaken all her wicked courses"

KING.

1. So-
2. Our
3. Our

- ci - e - ty has quite for - sak - en all her wick - ed cour - ses, Which emp - ties our po-
ci - ty we have beau - ti - fied—we've done it wil - ly nil - ly— And all that is - n't
Peer - age we've re - mod - ell'd on an in - tel - lect - ual ba - sis, Which cer - tain - ly is

FLOWERS OF PROGRESS.

- lice courts, and a - bol - ish - es di - vor - ces. Di - vorce is near - ly ob - so - lete in
Bel - grave Square is Strand and Pic - ca - dil - ly. We have - n't a - ny slum - mer - ies in
rough on our he - red - i - ta - ry ra - ces— We are go - ing to re - mod - el it in

England.
England !
England.

No to - le - rance we show to un - de - serv - ing rank and
We have solv'd the la - bour ques - tion with dis - crim - in - a - tion
The Brew - ers and the Cot - ton Lords no long - er seek ad

KING.

FLOWERS OF PROGRESS.

splen - dour ; For the high - er his po - si - tion is, the great - er the of - fen - der.
pol - ish'd, So pov - er - ty is ob - so - lete and hun - ger is a - bol - ish'd—
mis - sion, And Lit - e - ra - ry Me - rit meets with pro - per re - cog - ni - tion—

That's a
We are
As

KING.

max - im that is pre - va - lent in Eng - land.
go - ing to a - bol - ish it in Eng - land.
Lit - e - ra - ry Me - rit does in Eng - land.

No peer - ess at our
The Cham - ber - lain our
Who knows but we may

Draw - ing Room be - fore the Pre - sence pass - es
na - tive stage has purg'd, be - yond a ques - tion,
count a - mong our in - tel - lec - tual chick - ens

Who would - n't be ac - cept - ed by the
Of "risk - y" sit - u - a - tion and in -
Like you, an Earl of Thack - e - ray and

"So ends my dream"

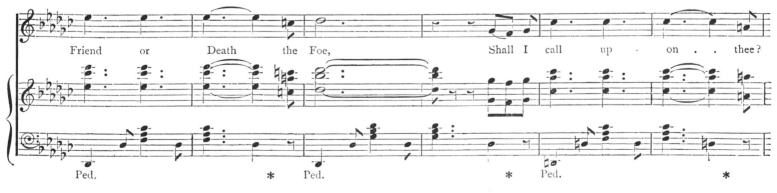

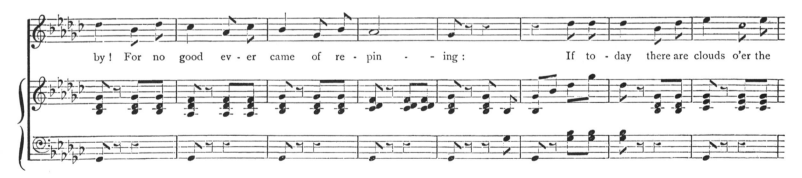

ser - vant, To - mo - row! God save you, To - mor - row! Your

ser - vant, To - mor - row! God save you! To - mor - row!

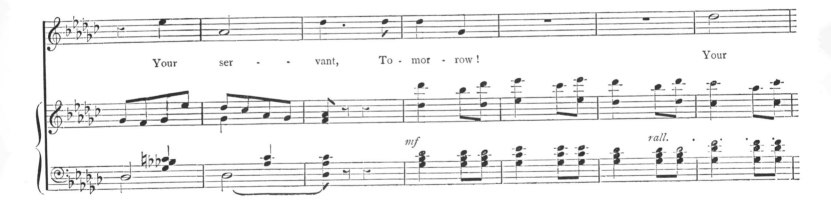

Your ser - - vant, To - mor - row! Your

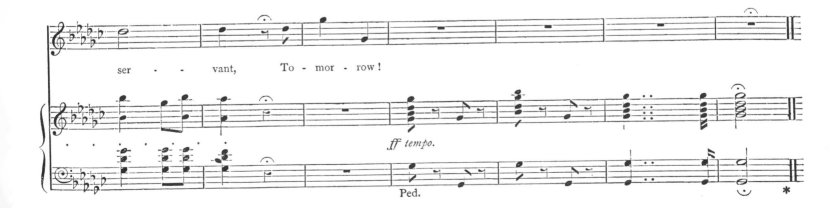

ser - - vant, To - mor - row!